Acadian Legends, Folktales, and Songs from
from
Prince Edward Island

by Georges Arsenault
translated by Sally Ross

Acadian Legends, Folktales, and Songs from Prince Edward Island

by Georges Arsenault
translated by Sally Ross

The Acorn Press
Charlottetown

2002

In memory of
Eleanor Wheler

Acadian Legends, Folktales, and Songs from Prince Edward Island
ISBN 1-894838-02-5

Cover Art: *Sunburst* by Karen Gallant, from a private collection
Book Design: Matthew MacKay
Printing: Williams & Crue (1982) Ltd., Summerside, PEI

The Acorn Press gratefully acknowledges the support of The Canada Council for the Arts, through its Translation Grants and Emerging Publishers Programs, as well as the Cultural Development Program of the Prince Edward Island Department of Community and Cultural Affairs.

National Library of Canada Cataloguing in Publication

Main entry under title :

   Acadian legends, folktales and songs from Prince Edward Island / compiled by Georges Arsenault ; translated by Sally Ross.

Translation of: *Contes, légendes et chansons de l'Île-du-Prince-Édouard.*
Includes bibliographical references.
ISBN 1-894838-02-5

      1. Folk literature, Canadian (French)—Prince Edward Island. 2. Folk songs, French—Prince Edward Island. 3. Canadians, French-speaking—Prince Edward Island—Folklore. 4. Acadians—Prince Edward Island--Folklore. I. Arsenault, Georges, 1952– II. Ross, Sally

GR113.5.P75C6513 2002   398.2'09717   C2002-902388-2

The Acorn Press
P.O. Box 22024
Charlottetown, Prince Edward Island
Canada C1A 9J2
www.acornpresscanada.com

Contents

Foreword

Back in my graduate-school days at Indiana University some forty-plus years ago, I took a course in "The Folktale" from the late Professor Warren Roberts, and practically his first assignment was that each of us should read and report on several hundred folktales of our own choosing. Knowing I'd be coming back to teach in Maine, and having already developed a strong interest in the Maritime Provinces of Canada, I decided to concentrate on French-Canadian material.

My "reading French" was pretty good back then, and I had a wonderful time working through the hundreds of tales, anecdotes, and legends collected by Marius Barbeau and others, and published by them in the early volumes of the *Journal of American Folk-Lore*. Among other things, I was fascinated to see how many of the *conteurs* claimed to have learned this-or-that story in the lumber-camps, often in Maine or New Hampshire. This assignment turned out to be one of the richest experiences of my graduate year. Better yet — and just for fun — almost every night I'd translate one of the stories I'd been reading and tell it to my eight-year-old son Steve. It was a great arrangement for both of us.

A bilingual narrator and an eager listener! It didn't occur to me at the time, but what Steve and I had there was the basic mechanism that allowed these folktales to move all over Europe — and wherever Europeans have moved — crossing from one language to another with relative ease. As a result, as Georges Arsenault is at pains to point out, it is no surprise that the same folktales he found on Prince Edward Island appear over and over in various European and Asian repertoires. Nor was I surprised to find that the several long folktales I collected from Wilmot MacDonald over on the Miramichi back in 1961 were extremely well-known in French Canada.

But when I turned my attention to French-Canadian ballads, I found that while they might share common themes, the English and French repertoires shared very little else — the same ballad in both languages was so rare as to be almost nonexistent. The reason was not far to seek: translating a song involves moving not just an idea, a story, but a text — a specific set of words in a tight order — from one metric (stanza form, rhyme, etc.) to another, and that requires someone sitting down and carefully working it out, line by line, stanza by stanza. It doesn't just "happen," as those stories I told Steve just happened. Small wonder, then, that it happened so seldom, and the songs chosen for the present collection demonstrate the consequence: not one of them has a direct parallel in English tradition.

Not only is poetic translation a difficult business, it is also, often enough, a thankless one, because any attempt at it is sure to jar the sensibilities of someone who knows the original. Sally Ross gives the illusion of treating this as a non-problem by keeping everything very straightforward and simple. Further, by attempting to make her English words fit the original French structures, she helps us experience how French balladry achieves its ends through forms and techniques quite different from those of English balladry. On a somewhat different level, since Ross also gives us the French texts along with the English, her line-by-line method has allowed someone like me — whose French has become rusty with years of disuse — at least a fighting chance to enjoy the originals. That is no small matter, and I thank her for it.

In much of what I have said up to this point lurks the idea that a song or a story is a thing in itself, existing, moving, and changing as though by its own rules, quite apart from any social or cultural context. That idea was central in my graduate school days, and, accordingly, studying a folksong or folktale meant researching its origin, history, distribution, and variation. No doubt about it, we learned a great deal from such studies, but many of us wanted more, and what we wanted was to put flesh and sinew on those dry bones. Who sang those songs or told those stories? To whom? When and under what circumstances? How were they performed, and how did those listening respond? In other words, what we wanted was that missing context, the human matrix that sustained these bare-bones texts and gave them life and meaning.

And that context is what Georges Arsenault has given us in this book. It is not a large or "definitive" collection, but it is a rich one because we get that matrix I spoke of. We meet the storytellers and singers themselves, and learn something of what the songs and stories meant both to them and to those who listened. We get a sense of the varied narrative styles and the vastly different social situations in which the stories were told (some in public gatherings to adults, some in the bosom of the family to children only). Some of the stories were accepted as factual accounts, others as fiction.

As for songs, rather than simply a collection of individual texts, we see them in two special contexts: first, a gleaning from one family's tradition; second, a collection of Island-made songs, showing that the old tradition, though changed and somewhat diminished, is still a presence to be reckoned with.

It has been a pleasure to read this book in manuscript. It will be an even greater pleasure to read it again when it appears between boards. Through it Georges Arsenault has done both the Acadian community and the whole of Prince Edward Island a great service, and it is my final pleasure to recommend his book to one and all. Enjoy!

Edward D. "Sandy" Ives
Bucksport, Maine

Preface

This book is a journey into the oral traditions of the Acadians on Prince Edward Island. I invite you to follow me on my voyage of discovery of the authentic singers and storytellers I met during the 1970s and 1980s. You might be surprised to learn, as I was, that the treasures of our Island heritage hidden in their memories were waiting to be rediscovered, even as they were gradually slipping deeper and deeper into oblivion. I will introduce you to some of the many Acadian men and women who welcomed me so warmly into their homes and who were willing to dust off the treasure chests of memory and share their wealth of legends, folktales, songs, and other gems from the past.

My voyage of discovery, which began in 1971 when I was a university student, led me into a world that was both foreign and familiar. Foreign because I had grown up in a village where radio and television had edged out storytellers and almost silenced traditional singers. Familiar because it was the world my parents and grandparents had lived in for a long time. Bits and pieces of the oral traditions from France had been preserved in my family's collective memory. I had a keen ear for any echoes from the past, and connected quickly to all the spoken traditions that these men and women were sharing with me, from the ballads of drowning men and the amazing tales of Ti-Jack to the fascinating stories of sorcerers. I was discovering my roots, my culture, and my traditions, which English-language radio and television had so successfully managed to stifle. These wonderful treasures were being transmitted to me in traditional Acadian speech, my mother tongue, with all its wonderful old French expressions.

Twenty-five years later, I am still amazed by the richness of these oral traditions that have been preserved for so long on the Island. How could one not marvel at the Chaisson family's huge repertoire of traditional songs, at the inexhaustible reserve of folktales of Délia Perry from Egmont Bay, and at the numerous and intriguing legends told by Emmanuel Gaudet from Harper Road?

Most of these traditions originated from France, the mother country of the Acadians. When the first pioneers settled in Acadie in 1604 and on the Island — formerly known as Isle Saint-Jean — in 1720, they brought with them from the Old World their heritage of legends, folktales, and songs that had been handed down from one generation to the next since time immemorial.

However, all these traditions did not arrive lumped together, frozen in time. Over the years, they have been altered, revised, and rejuvenated. The sea around an island helps protect its cultures, but it also facilitates contacts with the outside. In other words, the Acadians of Prince Edward Island have never been completely cut off from the rest of the world. History has shown that they moved around a great deal, often in spite of themselves, as was the case during the Deportation. After staying for varying lengths of time in France, on islands in the Gulf of St. Lawrence, in settlements along the coast of New Brunswick and elsewhere, many of the victims of the 1758 Deportation came back to Prince Edward Island to found new communities. After they returned, they maintained their ties with the outside world, especially with the Acadian communities in other regions where they often had relatives. As seamen and fishermen, many Acadians sailed to both near and distant shores, returning home with new stories and new songs.

From time to time, a boat would arrive in an Acadian village with a fisherman from a neighbouring province, a *Canadien* from Quebec or a *Français* from France, as they were called at the time. The contributions of all these people enriched the repertoire of the local singers and storytellers, always on the lookout for new material.

By the second half of the 19th century, the building of the railway enabled contingents of young Acadian men to leave Prince Edward Island for Nova Scotia, New Brunswick, or New England to work in the lumbercamps during the winter months. Whole families also left the Island to clear the land in the undeveloped parts of Quebec and New Brunswick, or to emigrate to the industrial cities of New England where they came in contact with Francophones and Anglophones from various places. The most adventurous Acadians went to the western United States, and even as far as the Klondike, to try their fortune. Undoubtedly, all of these voyages and contacts with people from elsewhere added to the oral traditions of the Acadian villages on the Island.

For centuries, Acadians have shared the Island with the Mi'kmaq, the English, the Scots, and the Irish. In fact, they have borrowed various elements from these different ethnic groups, not only in the area of songs, folktales, and legends, but especially in the non-oral traditions such as music, dance, and foodways.

After the British conquest, English quickly became the dominant language in every sector of life on Prince Edward Island, including the schools. The Gaelic language, whether Scottish or Irish, was the first to disappear, followed by Mi'kmaq. Although it fared a little better, French was not spared, and gradually it disappeared in the areas where the Acadians were numerically weak and intermingled with Anglophones. The French language was better able to withstand the pressure in the more homogeneous areas like the Evangeline Region. The majority of Acadians on the Island today do not speak the language of their ancestors. Although 25 per cent of the 134,557 inhabitants of the province claimed in 1996 to be either partly or entirely of French descent, at the time of the 1996 census only 5,718 Islanders, or 4.3 per cent of the total population, declared that French was their maternal tongue.

The singers and storytellers whom I interviewed and present in this book, however, grew up speaking French. In fact, the majority of them spoke French on a daily basis all their lives. Nevertheless, born between 1880 and 1936, they all spoke English, some more fluently than others.

All of these people did not speak French in exactly the same way; in other words, the number of English terms and the number of expressions typical of traditional Acadian French varied from one individual to another. The variations depended, for the most part, on the educational level of the individual and the vitality of the French spoken in his or her community.

I would like to express my warmest thanks to all the people who welcomed me so kindly into their homes, often on several occasions, and who were willing to share with me the vulnerable oral heritage that they had preserved for so long in their memory. Most of these individuals have now passed away, but, thanks to their generosity, they contributed, often without knowing it, to the preservation of an important treasure that is a source of pride for their descendants, and the Acadian community at large. We are profoundly grateful to them.

I wish to express my sincere thanks to Madame Florine Després, formerly with the Department of Music at the Université de Moncton, who transcribed the tunes of all the songs included in this work. I would also like to thank Jean Cormier who put the transcriptions on computer.

I am particularly grateful to the eminent folklorist Edward D. "Sandy" Ives, who kindly accepted to write the Foreword to this edition of my book. His research and publications have been a true source of inspiration. On various occasions over the years, I have had the opportunity to tell him about the research I was doing in a part of the Island that he, too, had explored. In fact, a few of my informants in West Prince met him long before I went to interview them.

I would also like to pay tribute to my friend Sally Ross, who translated this work celebrating Acadian oral traditions. She has captured with great sensitivity the many voices represented in this book. I would like to thank The Canada Council for the Arts, which has provided the translation grant that allowed this book to happen. Finally, I would like to express my sincere gratitude to Laurie Brinklow and The Acorn Press, which will now transmit these rich Island traditions to a broader audience.

Georges Arsenault
Charlottetown, 2002

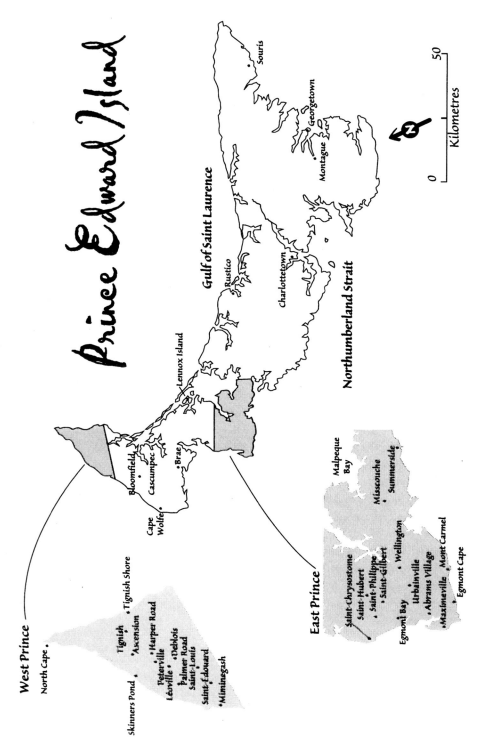

Prince Edward Island

Gulf of Saint Laurence

Souris

Georgetown

Montague

Rustico

Charlottetown

Northumberland Strait

Lennox Island

Bloomfield
Cascumpec
Brae
Cape Wolfe

West Prince

North Cape

Tignish Shore
Tignish
Ascension
Harper Road
Peterville
Leoville
DeBlois
Palmer Road
Saint-Louis
Saint-Édouard
Miminegash
Skinners Pond

East Prince

Malpeque Bay

Missoeuche
Summerside

Saint-Chrysostome
Saint-Hubert
Saint-Philippe
Saint-Gilbert
Wellington
Egmont Bay
Urbainville
Abrams Village
Maximeville
Mont Carmel
Egmont Cape

N

0   50
Kilometres

Chapter 1
Folktales

"On aurait pas grouillé pour notre vie."

Chapter 1 — Folktales

"On aurait pas grouillé pour notre vie."
"We wouldn't have budged for our lives."

In the days before electricity had reached the small villages of Prince Edward Island, an evening of storytelling was a privileged moment in people's lives. The image of a storyteller sitting in the kitchen, in the light of an oil lamp, remains engraved in the memory of everybody who can remember those days. "It was so quiet, you could have heard a mouse run across the floor," related Marcel Perry (1914–1997) from Peterville. "Us young folk would sit on the floor. We'd be there with our hands under our chin. We wouldn't have budged for our lives! It was wonderful to hear people talking like that."

Folktales once constituted a significant part of one's leisure time, especially in the off-season. First, there were the folktales that parents and grandparents told, tales such as *La Grande Barbounette, Poliplume, La Bête à sept têtes, Le sac de vérités*, and *Le loup et le renard*, which children would ask for over and over again. Born in Rustico in 1920, the writer Antoinette Gallant — along with her sisters — took great pleasure in listening to the popular tales her mother told:

> Right from the time we were little, my mother told folktales
> from the olden days. [...] They always began: *"Une fois d'même..."*
> ["There was once..."]. We knew them as well as our mother, she'd
> told them to us so often. Sometimes she'd be so tired in the
> evening that she'd try to skip a bit to make the story a little shorter.
> But we wouldn't let her miss a word. We'd say the word she'd tried
> to skip. We knew all the stories, but it was no fun telling them our-
> selves. It was much more interesting when she told them.[1]

Ozélie Boisvert (née Bernard, 1913–2002) grew up in the village of St. Edward. She, too, remembers the fairytales her mother told while knitting during long winter evenings. She would imitate all the characters, changing the tone of her voice, and making all the appropriate gestures. She always ended the story with the same sentence: *"...le gros loup m'a donnée un coup de pied vous savez où, et il m'a envoyée vous raconter toutes ces menteries".* ["...the big wolf gave me a kick in the you-know-what, and sent me to tell you all these lies."] Storytime was often associated with specific activities. According to Ozélie, "My sister and I would braid her long hair and make beautiful chignons; often she'd nod off because you fall asleep when someone plays with your hair."[2] Others remembered that their mother told folktales to make them keep still when she was giving them a bath or looking for lice in their hair.

In most families, there was at least one person who knew from memory the old folktales they told the children. Rare, however, were the real storytellers who went from house to house, or sometimes even from village to village, and who could keep an audience of all ages spellbound for a whole evening. As a rule, most villages had at least one of these popular entertainers. People still have fond memories of men such as Isidore Doucette from Ascension and his brother Jos ("Cadjo") Doucette from Harper Road; Jos Pascal Poirier (Perry) and Damien Arsenault from St. Edward; Aimé Aucoin from Mont Carmel; Jack Maxime Arsenault from Urbainville; and Alphonse (à Didace) Gallant from St. Hubert.

Because of their trade, some men became travelling storytellers. In Urbainville, for instance, "Péoche," as he was nicknamed, worked as a shoemaker by day and a storyteller by night. As Anita Chaisson, born in Tignish in 1925, explained to me:

> Usually the person who told stories was someone who could do
> all kinds of things. Sometimes he was a cobbler who could repair
> shoes and mend harnesses. So he wasn't just a storyteller. He went
> from door to door and people were very happy to see him coming.
> Many a time, he'd stay for a week at our house.

As soon as people knew there was a storyteller in the neighbourhood, they would hurry to find him, so that in no time the house would be filled with men, women, and children anxious to hear new stories. "In those days," as Marcel Perry told me, "that was our pastime in the evenings. Especially during Lent — that was the season for folktales. The storytellers would come here, we'd invite them. Sometimes they'd stay for three or four days before they moved on." The evening would start around seven or eight o'clock and end at midnight, or even later. On some occasions, there would be more than one storyteller at a time. They would take turns. In fact, they often became friends and would visit each other's villages and would be invited together for a session of folktales. This gave the storytellers themselves the opportunity to learn new stories.

They each had their own style. Concentrating on their facial expressions, the low-key storytellers spoke slowly and used gestures sparingly. They would breathe life into their tales by varying their delivery and the intonation of their voice, depending on the characters and the events. The extroverts or actors, on the other hand, would take the part of their characters and even stand up and move around the room for dramatic effect. Léo Gaudet, from Harper Road, considered this type of storyteller to be a "real" teller of tales: "It was just part of their nature. They'd make all the gestures and moves described in the story." He particularly appreciated Jos Doucette, commonly known as Cadjo:

He'd do all the movements. He'd be standing up and then he'd move here and there. If someone in the story was getting hit, he'd hit you. It was dangerous! But that's the way he did it. He'd act out everything in the story.

It appears that on one occasion, when he wanted to describe an episode of a man being thrown into prison, he actually opened a little door and pushed one of his listeners down into the cellar!

One might wonder where these stories that formed the repertoire of the old storytellers came from. As in the way of folksongs, many of the folktales originated in the Old World. In fact, the stories are much older than the songs because they can be traced back to the writings of antiquity. Created in different parts of Europe and the Near East, folktales spread as people migrated. The tale of *La Bête à sept têtes* (*The Dragon Slayer*), for example, was of French origin, but it travelled around Europe and Asia before reaching other continents. Obviously, when stories are adopted by other cultures and other languages, they change and take on local colour, hence the many and often very different versions of the same folktale.

Until the end of the 19th century, the greater part of the Acadian repertoire was probably comprised of folktales belonging to oral tradition. Prior to the 1850s, education was the privilege of a minority, and for a long time books were a rare commodity. Gradually, as schools developed, books became a little more accessible, and newspapers began to circulate in Acadian communities, storytellers, always looking for new tales, quickly turned to these written sources. Whenever a good book, such as Napoléon Bourassa's *Jacques et Marie* (1866), Canon Christophe Schmid's *Geneviève de Brabant*, or Father J.-B. Proulx's *L'enfant perdu et retrouvé* (1887), appeared in a village, it was not long before the storyteller would read it or have it read to him. Basilice Gallant (1885–1995) from Abrams Village recalled in particular *L'enfant perdu et retrouvé*:

> My father-in-law loved to read. He was incapacitated and unable to work, so he read in the daytime. In the evenings, we'd put the children to bed after they'd done their homework. He'd sit and tell us everything he'd read. Oh, what beautiful stories! There was the story *Les enfants perdus* [*L'enfant perdu et retrouvé*]… What beautiful stories!

Acadian storytellers also borrowed from English-language sources, such as the popular American series starring intrepid heroes such as Jesse James, Nick Carter, and Buffalo Bill. Amable Arsenault (1895–1982) from Tignish was particularly fond of this genre:

I remember when I was a young fellow [before the First World War], I would go somewhere where they sold books. I would buy books, the kind they called "wild west" or "cowboys." Oh, I loved them! There were wonderful stories in them. I'd read them, then, the next evening, I'd go tell people everything in the book.

Since many of the storytellers could not read, they were forced to resort to a reader. According to Anita Chaisson, those storytellers "added things and took out things to make really wonderful stories that you could listen to for two or three hours." Aldine Arsenault (1916–2000) said that this was the case for her uncle and neighbour, Jos Pascal Perry (Poirier) from St. Edward:

During Lent, my Uncle Jos Perry told stories. [His son-in-law] Grand Jos à Philias read books to him, then when the book was finished, after supper we'd see Uncle Jos coming. My mother would say "He's coming to tell a story." It was interesting. We wouldn't have budged. We'd listen to him all evening.

Sometimes the storyteller preferred to tell his story in several installments, stopping each evening at a strategic point, so as to build up suspense.

In addition to folktales and stories from literary sources, storytellers also expanded their repertoire by incorporating local legends, anecdotes, or personal adventures. Marguerita Richard (born in 1912) said that her father, Philias Doucette from Palmer Road, even went so far as to relate his dreams: "After he finished eating, he'd lie down on a couch somewhere and fall asleep. When he got up — he'd slept for maybe fifteen minutes — he'd have a long dream to tell us." Léo Gaudet from Harper Road remembers totally inventing a story that lasted for almost two hours: "One evening, they asked me to tell some stories, I didn't know any [new ones], I hadn't read any. So I made up one. I made it up as I went along. It was a nice story." It would appear that it had served its purpose since he never told it again.

Lazarette Gaudet (1909–1992)

Lazarette Gaudet from St. Edward was probably the last of the public story-tellers in the Acadian community on Prince Edward Island. During the 1970s, he was still able to find opportunities, although increasingly rare, during which he could spend an evening telling stories. He seemed to regret that he had lost his audience to television: "That's all gone nowadays. Since TV has come in, along with radios, all that's been abandoned. They're not interested in that anymore."

There was a time, however, when Lazarette could go around the village, easily finding several households ready to listen to his stories. Alice Jones (née Thibodeau), for example, remembered a time during her youth in the 1950s when Lazarette would appear at her house once or twice a week:

> That's what he'd do. He'd go from house to house telling stories.
> We believed everything he said. That's how we spent our evenings.
> There were about 12 of us in the house, including 10 children.
> We'd sit around the table, then Lazarette would sit at the end and
> tell us stories.

When electricity was installed in St. Edward in the late 1950s and early 1960s, people blew out their oil lamps and turned on their television sets. Lazarette soon realized that he could no longer compete with the small screen that was monopolizing his audiences. He would go on his regular rounds, but he would pass virtually unnoticed. "You'd go in, you'd say 'good evening' to them. You'd leave and say 'good evening' to them again. That's all. There was no conversation at all!" In those days, it was only on the odd occasion that he would be able to share his stories with a few friends who missed the storytelling of bygone days.

Son of Jérôme Gaudet and Émilie Poirier, "Lazarette à Jérôme à Lazare," as he was called, was born in St. Edward on July 11, 1909. He married his neigh-bour, Angéline Allain, in 1933, and they had three daughters. Carpentry was his main source of income, but he also fished and made Mi'kmaq-style baskets from ash.

Lazarette grew up surrounded by oral traditions. His father was a well-known storyteller and singer who was a member of the church choir. In fact, the Gaudets lived in a neighbourhood of St. Edward which was full of singers, musicians, and traditional storytellers. Some of the singers included members of the Chaisson family (see Chapter 3), one of whom being the storyteller and singer, Maggie Chaisson (née Gaudet), who was Lazarette's first cousin.

Lazarette had learned some of his stories from his father, but he stressed the fact that he had also heard them told by other people, in particular by his neighbours, Jim and Damien Arsenault. As Lazarette explained, many of his stories came from books that Fred Arsenault, Damien's son, read to them. "I'd go over there in the evening, then he'd read books. He couldn't tell stories, so I'd go back the next day and tell them." Lazarette was totally illiterate. He made a cross in lieu of a signature since he could not even sign his name.

Lazarette Gaudet in 1985
(Courtesy *West Prince Graphic*)

In addition to his talent as storyteller, Lazarette Gaudet was also known as the local genealogist. Thanks to his phenomenal memory, he could trace almost everyone's family tree and show that he was related to many people, albeit distantly by times.

Lazarette had proven himself as a public storyteller by the time he was 18 years old. He remembered evenings, before he was married, when he took part in storytelling sessions with his neighbours Jim and Damien Arsenault at the home of an elderly couple in the village. "We'd go there every evening to tell stories. They were thrilled to see us. They would have stayed up for months on end to listen to our stories. There was nothing else going on in those days."

Lazarette Gaudet's rich and varied repertoire included folktales as well as stories from books such as the adventures of Jesse James, legends, anecdotes about people of bygone days, and about his own personal experiences.

The following story, which Lazarette called *Pierre et Jules* ("Pierre and Jules"), belongs to the group of folktales about magic objects. In this particular case, it was a little mill that could produce on command anything that one desired. The tale in question is common throughout Europe, with the exception of France where it is little-known, which no doubt explains why so few versions of it have been collected in French Canada. Perhaps French Canadians learned it from Irish immigrants, since it is particularly popular in Ireland and Sweden. This tale has also been found as far away as China, Africa, and the West Indies.

—Pierre and Jules (Pierre et Jules) —

There were two brothers, one called Jules and the other called Pierre. And they each had their own farm. They were neighbours. Pierre was getting poorer and poorer, to the point where he was starving. As for Jules, he was getting richer and richer by the day.

One morning Pierre said to his wife, "There's no use, I've got to go away, I've got to find work. We're going to die of hunger," he said.

So he left. He walked all day. He walked and he walked. In the evening, at nightfall, he reached a forest. He hadn't gone very far when he saw a little cabin in the woods, with a little light. He was hungry and exhausted. He said to himself, "I've got to find a place for the night."

So he went to the cabin and knocked on the door. An old man saw him, then an old woman. The old man said, "Come in."

He went inside. And what did he find? An old man with a long beard that went all the way down to his knees. A huge white beard. "Sit down, young man, sit down. You look exhausted," he said.

"Well, yes," he said, "I am exhausted."

After he was seated, the old man said, "I imagine you're hungry."

"I haven't eaten today," Pierre replied.

"Well, get up and go over to the stove and you'll find some soup. I made a pot of soup. Help yourself."

Pierre was pleased. He got up and took a plateful of soup and began to eat. When he had finished, the old man said, "Now you won't be going any further tonight, you're too exhausted to walk any further. Make yourself a bed on the branches, like me, and go to sleep. No one will bother you."

Ah well, Pierre lay down, he was exhausted, totally exhausted. It seems he didn't move all night, he slept the whole night. The next morning, when he woke up, the old man was already up. "Good morning, Pierre," he said, "How are you?"

"Gee, you're smart, you know my name."

"Of course, I know everybody's name," he replied.

"Really?" said Pierre.

And he said, "I know where you're going. You're off to see if you can find work to support your family."

"Yes."

"Well," he said, "listen, I'm going to give you a little mill, then with that, you'll get everything you ask for! Food to eat, money, everything you'll need. I'll tell you the magic words to start it and to stop it. That's the secret."

Pierre thanked him nicely, then went on his way. In the evening, when he got back home, his wife said to him, "What have you got under your arm?"

"Say nothing," he replied.

He put it on the table and said to her, "Make a wish for food to eat."

Suddenly food appeared and the table was full of all kinds of food, as much as anyone could want.

"Now," he said, "we're going to eat. We haven't had a good meal for almost a year." Before they'd finished, he said, "Now, before we've finished eating, I want to see if what the old man told me is true." He put the mill back on the table and said, "I wish for money."

Suddenly money started coming out of the mill. Dollars and coins were pouring out and piling up on the floor!

"Oh," he said, "we're rich people now."

He stopped the mill.

With the money, he had all his buildings fixed up perfectly. Beautiful buildings they were. As a matter of fact, they were as nice as the buildings in the city.

"By geez!" his brother Jules said to his wife. "What's going on? My brother Pierre used to be so poor! They used to be starving! Look at the beautiful buildings he has. He's got hired hands and they've been working there for months. I'm going over to see what's going on."

Ah well! He was jealous.

He arrived there in the afternoon. "Pierre," he said, "what's happened? Where did you steal the money from? It would take a fortune to build buildings like those, they're so beautiful."

"Oh," he said, "it's nothing. It's this little mill."

"You've got to sell me that!"

"No, I'm not selling it to you, of course I'm not selling it to you!"

And Jules coaxed and coaxed. "I'll give you a thousand dollars," he said.

"No, no."

"I'll give you two thousand dollars."

"No."

"I'll give you three."

"I've got enough money now," Pierre thought to himself. "I'll let it go for three thousand."

"All right," he said, "I'll let you have it for three thousand."

He took the three thousand dollars cash and Jules took the little mill home. Pierre had shown him how to start it, but he hadn't told him how to stop it.

Jules had a hired hand who was clearing a piece of land at the back of the property. The next morning, Jules said to his wife, "We'll be coming home for dinner at noon. You'll have to have something to eat for dinner."

"All right," she said. And they left.

When ten o'clock came, or maybe ten-thirty, she said to herself, "I've got to make dinner for my husband and the young fellow he hired. They'll be here around eleven-thirty or twelve. What can I cook for them?" "Goodness," she thought, "it's been a long time since I've eaten fresh herring. I'll try for some herring."

Setting the little mill on the table, she said, "I wish for herring."

At that moment, herring started coming out of the mill. Herring poured out, filled up the house, and overflowed into the yard. She couldn't stop it. Her husband arrived. "Oh, gee!" he said, and ran over to Pierre's. He said to Pierre, "You've got to come over to our place! It's scary, all the herring."

Without leaving his house, Pierre said the magic words and the little mill stopped.

"This thing is no good to us," Jules said. "I could sell it to someone."

What's come in recently down on the shore? A big ship was from the mainland, you know. It brought in a load of stuff, and it was going to load up before it went back to the mainland.

There were twelve men on board. The captain said to his men when they'd finished unloading the cargo: "You can go in town now for the rest of the day. It'll be all right, providing you come back tonight, so when the tide's high, we can leave."

In those days, there was no such thing as a boat run by gas, it was all sails, you know.

The men promised him they'd be back in time. So they all left.

After they left for town, the captain thought to himself, "I should go for a walk in town myself to see what it's like. I've never been to this place before."

He left the ship and wandered here and there. It wasn't long before he heard about the little mill. He asked who owned it. And people told him. "I must go and see," he thought.

Oh yes! He arrived at Jules' place in the afternoon, around two or three o'clock. He was tired. Oh well.

"Hello."

"Hello."

The captain said to Jules, "I was sent here. Someone told me today that you had a little mill that you could get all kinds of things from, like money, food…"

"Ah, that's true," he said, "that's true."

"Well, you must show it to me."

"I won't show it to you, I'll sell it to you if you want," he said, "cheap."

"Really? How much?"

"Give me what I paid for it and take it away. I paid three thousand dollars for it."

The captain had enough money, so he bought it. Jules showed him how to start it.

That was fine. He took it back to the ship.

In the evening, the crew was back on board, ready to set sail during the night. There were twelve men, not counting the captain. One of them called to him and said, "What's that you've got there?"

"Say nothing," he said, "I'm going to use it soon."

Well, they had come here for a load of salt. The captain said, "We don't need to buy salt, the little mill says we're going to have some."

Then, he set it up in a corner of the ship. The captain said to the little mill, "Now, we want salt."

At that moment, salt started coming out of the mill, and then more salt and more salt. There was so much that it started pouring overboard and the captain couldn't stop it. The ship sank and that's why today the sea is salty.[3]

Lazarette Gaudet spoke quickly and told his stories in a rhythmical and lively way. He never burdened his narrative with descriptions or psychological details, and he knew how to create dialogue — signs of a teller in full command of his art.

The structure of the following tale is based on a series of riddles. The word for riddle in Acadian French is *dévine*, hence Lazarette's title. Like the preceding folktale, this one is also well-known and well-travelled. Folklorists believe that riddles originated in India.

— The Riddles (Les dévines) —

There once was an old man and an old woman who lived together with their two sons. One was called Tom and the other was a lazybones called Jack. They were living on their landlord's farm. Every year, he'd come to collect his rent. It had to be paid every year. But one year when he came, they didn't have a cent, not a penny. The man said to them, "I'll let it go for another year. If you can't pay, well…" And so off he went.

He came back the next year. There was still no money. So he said to them, "I'll give you one more chance. That'll be three years. If you can't pay then, you'll have to leave. It's my land." And off he went.

Time passed and the days went by. They planted crops. They put in potatoes, they put in oats, they put in wheat, to make flour for the winter, you understand. They planted a little garden for themselves.

The day before the landowner was due to arrive, the old woman said to her old man, "Did you save some money to pay our rent?"

"I haven't got a cent," he said, "not a penny."

So she said, "We might as well start packing our clothes. Tomorrow we'll have to leave. You know what he said three years ago."

Little Jack, who was sitting behind the stove, said, "Mother, don't hurry. I'll tell you what to do. Tomorrow morning, hide in a room with Father and my brother Tom. I'll take care of everything."

"Oh well," the old woman said, "we might as well listen to him. We're going to have to leave anyway."

The next morning, after they'd done the chores, the three of them hid in a room. Jack was sitting behind the stove. Soon, nine o'clock came and there was a knock at the door. He knew who it was.

"Come in," he said. So the landlord came inside.

Jack said, "Pull up a chair and sit down." The landlord sat down and said, "What are you doing?"

"Ha! What am I doing?" Jack replied.

"Where's your father?"

"My father's gone to get the good out of the better."

"Gosh," he thought to himself. "What does the good out of the better mean. Oh well."

"And where's your mother?"

"My mother went to do for other women what she can't do for herself."

"This is getting worse," he thought. "And your brother?"

"My brother has gone hunting. Whatever he kills he leaves behind, and whatever he doesn't kill, he brings back."

The landlord sat there. He was stuck. He couldn't solve the three riddles. "Listen, Jack," he said, "tomorrow morning, come to my office in town. Don't come naked, dressed, on horseback, or on foot." And he left.

No sooner had he left when the others came out of the room. "Hey, you're going to get it, Jack."

"Ah, don't worry."

The next day after he'd had breakfast, he said, "Now I've got to go see the landlord." He left. Not far from the house, there was a river. A big river, you understand. He thought he'd go down to the river to wash. He probably hadn't washed for a year. When he got there, he saw the end of a net sticking out of the water. Someone must have left the net there, maybe to catch trout or something. He pulled it up on the sand. He started examining it. "Well," he said to himself, "if I take my clothes off, I can wrap myself in this. It's not clothes and I wouldn't be naked."

So that's what he did. He took off his clothes and wrapped himself in the net. He looked at himself and said, "Gee! I'm not naked and I'm not dressed."

Now, he couldn't go on horseback and he couldn't walk. He headed out the road to go to the town. It was a couple of miles. When he was about halfway, he saw a bunch of sheep. There was big nasty-looking ram. Geez, he headed straight for him. He walked up to the ram, grabbed him by the horns, turned him around and got on his back. With a kick here and a kick there, he drove him along the road. He drove him right up to the landlord's door. The landlord came out. He watched and he saw him coming. "Geez," he said, "he's coming here."

"Well," said Jack, "am I on horseback?"

"No."

"Am I on foot?"

"No."

"By God," he says, "I'm not naked and I'm not dressed."

"No," the landlord said. "Let the ram go and come inside." He led him into his office, then he brought him some clothes. Jack put on the clothes.

"Sit down. Well, now look here. When I came back from your place yesterday, I looked in my books. I didn't sleep all night, not a wink." Then he said, "I couldn't solve the riddles you told me. You said your father had gone to get the good out of the better. Well, what does that mean?"

"Ha! that's easy," Jack said. "You know that beef is good to eat in the fall."

"Yes."

"Well," he said, "wheat is better still. You can make flour with it. Well, when my father got up in the morning, there was a bull in the wheat field on your property. So he went to get it out of the wheat. He went to get the good out of the better."

"By God," he said, "you're right, Jack. That's true. Then, you told me your mother went to do for other women what she can't do for herself."

"That's easy, too. When my mother's giving birth, she can't deliver the baby all alone, eh! But when another woman is giving birth, she can go and help deliver the baby. The other night, she'd been called to go and take care of a woman who was having a baby."

"Well, Jack, you're smart. But that's not the worst. You told me that your brother went hunting and that what he kills he leaves behind, and what he doesn't kill he brings home."

"That's really easy," Jack said. "My brother has lice. Every morning he goes off to the woods, then he takes off his clothes and kills lice all day. Well, the ones he kills, he leaves behind and the ones he doesn't kill, he brings back on his clothes."

With that, the landlord said, "Jack, go away. I'll never bother you again."

And he gave him a clear receipt on the property. So Jack had won him over.[4]

Délia Perry (1899–1967)

Public storytellers, such as Lazarette Gaudet, who went from house to house telling their tales, were almost always men. On Prince Edward Island, however, there was one exception and that was Délia Perry (Poirier) from Egmont Bay parish.

Daughter of Joseph Gallant and Marie Arsenault, Délia Perry was born in the village of St. Chrysostome on July 24, 1899. She attended the little village school for seven years. Before she was married, she worked as a maid in 28 different households, and lived for a short while in Chelsea, Massachusetts, and in Rogersville, New Brunswick. At the age of 31, she married the widower Dan Perry (Poirier), a barber and carpenter from Summerside, who had four children. Délia Perry had eleven children, two of whom died shortly after they were born.

Délia Perry, around 1955 (Auldine Huot Collection)

Délia had a happy marriage, but after the death of her husband in 1949, she found herself alone at the age of 50 with virtually no income and a large family to raise. A month before her husband Dan died, the entire family had moved to St. Chrysostome. As Evelyn Babineau, one of her daughters stated, the move to the countryside where there was no electricity proved to be a culture shock for the children. They had all grown up in Summerside where houses and streets had had electric lights for years.

> I remember the evening we moved to Egmont Bay. We were nine children. They led us upstairs by lamplight in our bedroom. We cried almost all night long. My mother left a lamp lit. We slept like that for a year with the lamp on.

Délia's children have no recollection of their mother telling stories when they were living in Summerside, at least not at home. She took up the tradition after her husband's death. It was around then that she started visiting families in the neighbourhood to tell stories that she had learned mainly from her mother and an older brother, "André the Blind," who was well-known as an excellent storyteller. Délia's daughter, Auldine Huot, recalled one occasion in particular when she accompanied her mother for an evening of storytelling:

> Even today, when I think about it, I wonder how she could re-
> member all of that because the story lasted the whole evening, two
> hours. And the way she told it! You couldn't take your eyes off her
> when she was speaking. You'd ask yourself, "What's she going to
> say next? And what's going to happen next?" It was so real, so vivid.

In 1957, the folklorist Luc Lacourcière from Laval University had the good fortune to meet this prolific storyteller when she was living near the church in Egmont Bay. She told him that one winter she had gone around all the houses in the village telling stories. She said she never went out more than three times a week because she didn't want to be taken for a man-hunter! Over the course of a number of recording sessions in 1957 and 1958, Professor Lacourcière collected 90 of the 100 tales or stories in Délia Perry's repertoire. These included folktales and stories based on books she had read and serials she had found in *L'Impartial*, the Acadian newspaper published in Tignish from 1893 to 1915. When she was young, she had read a great deal in both English and French to André, her blind brother.

Délia Perry was a good storyteller whose narrative style was very different from that of Lazarette Gaudet. She spoke slowly, choosing and articulating her words carefully. She had good control of dialogue, but it was not as animated or direct as Lazarette's. She tended to give her characters longer lines. In addition, there was a marked difference between the level of language of the two storytellers. Although she used many expressions typical of the Acadian dialect,

Délia spoke a much more standard French without any English words at all. However, I should point out that she was telling her stories to a university professor from Quebec, who, from her point of view, would be speaking very eloquently. Consequently, it would be normal for her to use her very best French.

Délia Perry's stories vary in length from about a half an hour to a few minutes. The following story, *Le grand devineur (The Great Soothsayer)*, is of average length and is a very well-known folktale thought to be of Asian origin since it has been found in ancient collections of Buddhist tales published in India. Délia was 59 years old when she told this story to Professor Lacourcière, on August 12, 1958.

— The Great Soothsayer (Le grand devineur) —

There was once an old man and an old woman. They lived in the country. And they didn't know what to do to make a living. They were too old to work, people weren't very charitable — although it has to be said that everybody was poor — and they had no one to help them. One day the old man said to his wife, "I think we're going to die of hunger. We won't live long."

"I agree," the old woman replied. "In a month's time, there will be nothing left to eat. There's no way of finding any more food. We've got to do something. What can we do to survive?"

One day the old man had an idea. "We'll put in the papers that we're good soothsayers, great soothsayers, and that there's nothing we can't foresee. People will come here, famous people with lots of money. Then, when they discover that we can't foresee anything, they won't need us and they'll kill us. We won't have to starve and suffer for a month. They'll kill us and that'll be the end. I think that's the best plan for dying right away."

"Well," said the old woman, "that's a good plan. We won't be able to foresee anything, so they'll kill us and that'll be the end."

"Good!" said the old man. He had an announcement put in the paper that they were great soothsayers. There was nothing they couldn't foresee.

Four or five days passed. One day, what do you think happened? Someone was sent by the king. The king sent for them. They got ready and put on the best clothes they could find. And off they went.

"Is it true that you are good soothsayers, the best soothsayers in the world?" the king asked them.

"Yes," replied the old man, "definitely."

"Well," said the king, "I'm going to put you in a big room for three days. You will only be given one meal a day, your dinner. It will be a good meal.

Then, at the end of three days, I will have everyone in the city come and you will go up on a platform and you will tell everyone what I am going to ask you to foresee. And that will be to say where my daughter's ring is. My daughter lost her ring several days ago. We can't find it anywhere."

"Very good," said the old man.

The next day at noon, the king's servant brought them their dinner. It was a beautiful big dinner. They ate. The servant watched them while they ate.

After they had finished eating, the old man turned to his wife and said, "That's the first one!"

He meant the first meal before they were going to die.

The servant came back. It seems that it was the king's three servants who had stolen the ring. Then he left and went to the other two servants. "I think we've been caught," he said to them. "The old man's guessed because he said to his wife, 'That's the first one!' I'm not serving them dinner again. You can go," he said to one of the other servants.

The next day at noon, another servant took them their dinner. After the old man had finished eating, once again he turned to his wife and said, "That's the second one!"

The servant went to find the other king's servant. He said to him, "I'm not going back there again. He's guessed me, too. We've been caught."

The third servant said, "I'll go."

On the third day, he took them their dinner. Once again the old man turned to his wife and said, "And that's the third one! The third and last one."

Oh, they were frightened, the king's servants. They said, "The old man and the old woman have guessed that it's us. What are we going to do? The king will have us put to death. We'll not only lose our place here, our work, he'll have us put to death. What can we do?"

It was the next day that the old man and the old woman were supposed to say who had taken the ring, to say what had become of the king's daughter's ring.

The next morning, the three servants went to see the old man and the old woman. They said to them, "We know you've guessed that we stole the king's daughter's ring."

Not letting on that he was surprised, the old man said, "Yes."

"What can you do, so as not to tell the king that it was us? We'll be hanged," they said.

"Ah, well," the old man said, "for that, you'll have to bring me the ring. I'll take care of things."

"If you want to take care of things," they said, "we'll not only give you the ring, but each one of us will give you one hundred dollars, so that the king won't find out that it was us."

When everybody was ready and everyone was there, the old man and the old woman arrived. The king had them go up on the platform.

"Now," said the king, "where is my daughter's ring?"

The old man said, "One of your big turkeys, the biggest one, ate it."

"Oh! you're joking," said the king.

"Well, if you're afraid to kill your big turkey," said the old man, "it's not my fault. Kill your big turkey and you'll find the ring."

The king sent for his servants. "Kill the big turkey, the biggest one," the king said.

The big turkey was killed and the ring was inside it.

The old man had taken a little piece of bread, put the ring in it, and thrown it outside. Then he watched. It was the biggest turkey that had eaten it. The ring was inside the big turkey.

The king had to give them all the money he'd promised them. He'd told them he would have them killed. But there was a big sum of money if they could say where the ring was. The three servants had already each given them one hundred dollars.

The old man and the old woman went home and they lived to be as old as they wanted.[5]

Léah Gallant (1899–1984)

The tradition of storytelling in public was predominantly the domain of men, whereas the tradition of storytelling in the home belonged primarily to women. In most cases, it was the mother or grandmother who told children the stories she had heard from her parents. This domestic tradition lasted much longer than the evenings of storytelling since it only involved one adult and one or more children. In the early 1970s, for example, the storyteller Léah Maddix (1899–1986) was still passing on many of her wonderful tales to her grandchildren and friends.[6]

Although less prolific than Léah Maddix, Léah Gallant from Abrams Village had a clear recollection of many of the folktales her mother often told, including *Le petit cheval qui chie de l'argent*, *La chatte*, *Tom tout nu*, *Poliplume*, *Tom et Ti-Jack*, and *La chatte blanche*. At the age of 74, Léah Gallant had no difficulty remembering these stories because she had continued telling them to her grandchildren whenever they visited her or whenever she went to see them in Quebec or Massachusetts. She spoke English fluently and would even translate her stories for children who could not understand French.

Daughter of Daniel and Balthilde Arsenault, Léah Gallant was born on November 16, 1899, in the little village of Maximeville. She attended school in her native village and in Abrams Village before obtaining her teacher's licence from Prince of Wales College in Charlottetown. Before she married Cyrus Gallant from Abrams Village, she taught for eight years and then again for several years after her three children had left home.

Léah Gallant with her grandchildren in 1958
(Corinne Berthiaume Collection)

The following story, called *La chatte blanche* (*The White Cat*), belongs to the category of folktales involving a quest or a difficult task to accomplish. In this case, three brothers compete for the hand of a princess. It is a folktale that has spread throughout Europe, western Asia, North Africa, and Canada. In this version, beautifully told by Léah Gallant, one can recognize the form and style of the classic fairytale with the characteristic triple repetitions and typical expressions such as "a year and a day" and "in fairytales, time flies."

— The White Cat (*La chatte blanche*) —

There was a king. His wife was dead, so he lived alone with his daughter. He was beginning to get old, so one day he said to his daughter, "You should get married so there will be someone to inherit the throne."

That was nice, she was happy.

In those days, it was the father who chose a husband for his daughters. The king announced that he was looking for a young man to marry his daughter. As a result, young men starting coming, but he turned them away, one after another. Finally, there were three. He didn't know which of the three he should choose. So he said to them, "I'm going to send you to look for a rug to put in my castle. The one who brings me the most beautiful rug will have my daughter's hand in marriage. I'll give you a year and a day."

Well, they were three brothers. So they said to him, "Jack won't be coming (the youngest brother was called Jack), he won't be coming."

"Oh!" said the king, "that's all right, he won't bring back the most beautiful rug anyway."

"He'll only have the old white mare," they said.

Jack said, "That's okay. I'll be happy with the old white mare."

So off they went. And for a while the old white mare was smart and kept up with the others. But when they went into a forest, she didn't want to go any further. So Jack said, "Well, continue on, my brothers. I'm going to take a little path in the woods. My old mare doesn't want to go fast to keep up with you."

So the others continued on their way and he took a little path in the woods. Soon he came to a mud hole. The old white mare got stuck in the mud. "Oh," he thought, "we might as well stay here."

Jack jumped on her back to push her deeper into the mud. What's that? A big white cat. "Hey! hey! hey!" she said to him. "What are you doing? Burying your mare? Get her out of there."

"Oh," he said, "she doesn't want to walk anymore."

"But get her out of there, then come to our place. I'm sure that when you leave, you'll have a nicer rug than your brothers."

Well, he was surprised that the cat knew all that. He thought to himself, "Even if she only gives me mice to eat, I'm going with her if she wants to give me a beautiful rug."

So he went to the cat's house with the old white mare. He tied her up and then the cat said, "Put her in the barn and give her some hay and some oats, then come to the house."

He put his mare in the barn, took care of her nicely, and then went to the house. The cat had a good supper for him and time passed quickly. In fairytales, time flies, doesn't it!

When the time came to go home, she said to him, "Tomorrow morning, when you get up, there will be a little box on the table. Take the box, then hurry and catch up with your brothers."

So the next day, just as the cat had said, there was a little box on the table. He took it, then he went to the barn. He got his old white mare ready. She was fat! He got on her back and rode off.

When he reached the mud hole, this time the old white mare didn't get stuck in the mud. She was quick, she was galloping. When he reached the end of the road, he saw his brothers racing along in front of him. So he kept on going, and then they arrived at the castle. He let his brothers go in first.

The first one went in and showed his rug to the king. The king found it very beautiful. The next brother went in and also showed his rug to the king. The king found it very beautiful. Then Little Jack went in. He gave his little box to the king, saying, "This was given to me, I haven't even looked inside to see what's in the box."

So the king opened the box and spread the rug out on the floor. Oh! he'd never seen such a beautiful rug. "Jack's is the most beautiful," he said.

But it was hard for him to give his daughter to Jack. So he said, "Well, I am going to give you another chance. I will give my daughter to the one who brings me the most beautiful little dog, the most beautiful and the most gentle."

The brothers left the next morning. Once again Jack took his old mare. When he arrived at the little path, he said to his brothers, "I'm going this way."

Well, of course the others didn't know where he had found the rug, so they continued on their way, and Jack went off to find the big white cat. She was really happy to see him. She said, "That's right, when you go back, I promise you that you'll have a more beautiful dog than your brothers."

He found it funny that she knew everything the king had said.

Once again, time flew by, and the night before he had to leave, the white cat said, "Tomorrow morning, you will get up early and you will take the little box and leave."

So the next morning, he took the little box, then got his old mare ready. She was pretty smart. When he reached the end of the little path, he met his brothers who were on their way back. So he arrived at the castle at the same time as his brothers, but he let them go in first. They each showed their little dogs. They were beautiful and gentle little dogs.

Then Jack went and gave his little box to the king. He said to the king, "I haven't even looked inside to see what's in the box. It was given to me."

The king opened the box. A beautiful little dog jumped out onto the floor, bowed to the king, and then jumped up on his lap.

Ah! The king was delighted. He said, "Once again, Jack's is the most beautiful. Well, I am going to give you one last chance and, if Jack wins, he will have my daughter. He who finds me the most beautiful and the politest girl. And this will be the last time."

So they left the next morning. Jack thought to himself, "Where will the cat find a girl? Oh well!" he said, "I'll go and see her because she's been good to me up to now."

He went there. Once again she was happy to see him. She said, "Put your old mare in the barn, give her something to eat, then come to the house."

So the year flew by, a year and a day. The night before he had to leave, the white cat said, "Now come with me to the brook."

They went to the brook. She said, "Now, I am going to put my neck on the block and you will cut off my head."

"Oh! goodness no! You've been far too kind to me. I don't want to cut off your head."

"Yes, you have to cut off my head or else I'll cut yours off."

"Ah well! Rather than have you cut off my head, I'll have to…"

"Yes, cut off my head, then wash it in the brook, then stick it back on. Tomorrow morning, get up early."

Oh! It distressed Little Jack to cut off her head, but he had to.

He cut off her head, then he washed it as best he could, then he put it back on. Then he went back to the house to go to bed.

The next morning, when he got up, sitting on the table in the hall was the most beautiful girl he'd ever seen. She said, "Hurry, go to the barn. You'll find new clothes and a new horse. Get dressed. Hurry, we're going to leave."

With that, he went to the barn and changed into his new clothes. There was a beautiful horse and a beautiful shiny saddle. He put the harness on the horse, then he went to the house. The girl got up on the horse with him and they left.

When he reached the end of the little path, he saw his brothers coming. He said, "We'll let my brothers go first." So he let them pass him and he followed behind.

While the brothers were away, the king had something installed on the door, so that when they entered the girl's hat would be knocked off. So when they arrived, the oldest one went in with his young girl. When he entered, her hat fell off.

"What's this?" she said. She picked up her hat and went over to curtsy and present her hand to the king. The king thought she was quite polite.

Well, the next brother entered and his young girl's hat also got caught and fell off. The young girl said nothing, picked up the hat, went over to curtsy and present her hand to the king, then she spoke.

The king thought to himself, "This one is a little politer."

Next, Jack's young girl entered, then her hat also got caught and fell off. But she left her hat on the floor, went over to curtsy and presented her hand to the king. She spoke to him and then she said, "Excuse me, my hat fell off when I came in, I must go and pick it up."

"Well," said the king, "Once again it's Jack. His young girl is the politest and the most beautiful."

With that, Jack said, "No, I don't want your daughter, I'm going to marry this young girl."

So they got married. Now, I don't know which of the two other brothers married the king's daughter. It was one of the two who married his daughter. Jack and his young girl went to their castle because she was a pretty princess who had been turned into a cat by a wicked fairy. And it was only after having her head cut off that she could become a princess again.[7]

Emily Blacquiere (born in 1917)

Emily Blacquiere from Summerside grew up in Maximeville, where she was born not far from her cousin Léah Gallant. Born on January 30, 1917, Emily was the tenth of Marie and Léon Arsenault's 15 children.[8]

Unlike her cousin Léah, Emily Blacquiere had forgotten almost all the folktales her mother used to tell so beautifully. However, she had many happy memories of the wonderful times she and her brothers and sisters had spent in the company of fascinating characters such as Ti-Jack, Jean le Sot, Ti-Poucet, Mère à grand'dent, and Marlèche, who inhabited the imaginary world their mother told them about so often. Emily could still remember very clearly her mother, a seamstress, sitting by the stove making buttonholes and telling wonderful tales full of adventures.

Emily Blacquiere in 1997 (photo by Georges Arsenault)

In 1975, when she was 57 years old, Emily managed to recall, with the help of an older sister, one of the animal stories from their mother's repertoire. It was a folktale called *La Marlèche* (*Mrs. Blackbird*), which is actually comprised of two short animal stories. In the first one, a fox catches a dog called Roubi stealing eggs from a blackbird's nest, and, in the second one, a dog is caught in the cellar where he went to steal food. The first story has only been collected in the Acadian areas of Canada, and most of the versions have been found in the Evangeline Region of Prince Edward Island. It has also been found in Europe, particularly in France. The second story is well-known in French Canada and throughout Europe.

It would appear that the story of the blackbird, *La Marlèche*, and the dog, Roubi, was so well-known among Island Acadians that the characters became part of everyday speech. In fact, parents often referred to the blackbird when they wanted to scare children who misbehaved. A young girl or a woman who was somewhat shameless or even pretentious was called a *grande marlèche*. When a child did something clever, one would say, *Ah! toi, ma petite marlèche!* (Ah! you clever little blackbird!). In some families, instead of saying "to freeze one's nose," one would say *geler la marlèche* (to freeze one's blackbird). One day, during a conversation about the impact of television on people's social lives, I heard someone say, *Asteure, on s'embarre dans la maison à regarder la TV comme une marlèche* (Nowadays you get tangled up in the house watching TV like a blackbird). Some Island Acadians also remember people who were nicknamed *Marlèche*. Roubi the Dog appears less frequently in local expressions than the *marlèche*, but in Mont Carmel, for example, a naughty child is often called *petit chien Roubi* (little dog Roubi).

— Mrs. Blackbird (La Marlèche) —

There was once a blackbird who lived all alone. She was a widow. One fine day, she said to herself, "Gosh, what a beautiful day to go and visit my neighbour." So she got dressed and went out.

Roubi the Dog, who had seen her take off, said to himself, "Gosh! Mrs. Blackbird's gone out, I'm going to see if she's got eggs hidden anywhere."

He went into her house, looked around, and found a basketful of eggs. Oh, he was happy. He got the frying pan, lit the fire, and began to fry himself some eggs. He fried a few eggs, then he fried some more. Then he began to eat. He ate and he ate and he ate until he was so full he collapsed on the floor and fell asleep. He slept and snored all day long.

When he woke up, it was almost dark. He thought to himself, "I've got to get on my feet and take to the woods, because if Mrs. Blackbird comes back and finds me here, she'll kill me!" He ran off.

It wasn't long before Mrs. Blackbird came back. When she looked at her stove she saw the dirty frying pan. Someone had been frying eggs. "That's funny, I didn't leave the frying pan on the stove," she said to herself. "I must go and check my eggs."

She went to look at her eggs and discovered that they were all gone! At that point, she burst into tears, "Chirlip, chirlap, chirlip, chirlap."

All of a sudden, a fox, who was passing by, said, "Poor Mrs. Blackbird, why are you crying?"

She said, "I laid eggs for the winter, but unfortunately I went out visiting today and someone came and ate all my eggs."

"Well," said the fox, "I have an idea who might have done that. I saw Roubi the Dog roaming around. He's so bold, you know. I wouldn't be surprised if it were him."

"Now," she said, "I won't have any eggs for winter."

"Hey!" he said, "I think I know what we could do to catch him. If you lay some more eggs, I'm sure he'll come back for more."

So Mrs. Blackbird sat on her nest for a couple of days and laid some eggs. One night the fox hid and was watching for Roubi the Dog. All of a sudden, Roubi the Dog arrived, then the fox jumped out and caught him. He said, "There, I've caught you now. It was you who stole Mrs. Blackbird's eggs and now you're bold enough to come back to steal more. We're going to eat you."

"Well," the dog replied, "if you don't eat me, I'll tell you where there're lots of eggs. If you like, I'll go and get you as many as you need for the winter."

Mrs. Blackbird said to the fox, "Oh well, he's not very fat, so if he wants to go and get us some eggs, then we'll let him go. We'll let him live."

So the dog ran off to a farm where he knew there were lots of eggs. He came back with a basketful. Oh! Mrs. Blackbird was happy! The fox said, "Now wouldn't it be nice if we had some bacon to go with the eggs."

"I know where there's lots of bacon," said Roubi the Dog. "I'll go and get some." So off he went to the farmer's house to get some bacon. By this time, the farmer had noticed that there were eggs missing. He suspected that it was Roubi the Dog who had stolen the eggs. "He stole our eggs," the farmer said, "he'll come back to get bacon to go with them." So he put his big dogs down in the cellar.

Roubi the Dog went down into the cellar. When he got down there, two dogs caught him. Then the farmer went down into the cellar and said, "It was you who stole our eggs, and now you're bold enough to come and steal our bacon. We're going to kill you!"

They took him outside, hitched the oxen to his legs and they ripped him to pieces.

25 — Georges Arsenault

And so Mrs. Blackbird lived happily every after. When I passed by the other day, she was sitting on her nest singing, "Chirlip, chirlap, chirlip, chirlap."[9]

Delphine Arsenault (1912–1983)

The repertoire of folktales includes much more than the intricate stories I have quoted thus far. There are also innumerable tales and anecdotes based on a single theme, often told in the form of a joke. Although "professional" storytellers would include them in their evenings of storytelling, one does not have to be an experienced storyteller to tell these short tales or *petits contes*, as they are called, since they are easy to learn and easy to remember. These funny stories can be told quickly in all kinds of situations, while waiting in line at the grocery store or for the bingo game to start. Needless to say, Acadians still enjoy jokes, as do other Islanders.

Delphine Arsenault, around 1960
(Charlie Arsenault Collection)

As a rule, the jokes are meant for adult audiences, since they often contain sexual innuendos. The jokes talk about married couples, bachelors, priests, and even simple-minded or foolish people. These short tales also include anecdotes describing amazing feats and tales of lying.

One might think that some of these stories are of recent and local fabrication when, in fact, they are of very distant origin in both time and space. Some have been modified and modernized, whereas others have been handed down virtually intact. There is an anecdote in the Acadian repertoire on the Island related to a feeble-minded woman who tried to hatch a pumpkin because she thought it was a mare's egg! That ridiculous story might well have been invented locally. In fact, it appears in ancient books of Turkish fables and is told throughout Europe, most of Asia, and in North and South America.

Delphine Arsenault[10] from Summerside loved to tell anecdotes. Born on April 23, 1912, in Abrams Village, she was a member of the well-known musical family called the "Jos Bibienne." Her parents were Jos Arsenault and Julianne LeClair. Although she was best-known as a fiddler, Delphine also played the harmonica and the harmonium. She was an excellent stepdancer and a good singer who knew a number of folksongs.

This multi-talented woman could tell jokes and anecdotes of all kinds. It is amazing to realize that the following fish story about Gus Maddix and his friends is a very old tall tale that has been found throughout Scandinavia and many other countries.

— Eel Fishing (La pêche à l'anguille) —

Do you remember old Gus Maddix? He was always bragging. He always did everything better than everyone else, everything better than everyone else.

We were talking about fishing one day. And he said, "We were out fishing eels. Boy o'boy! Did we have a good catch. We tried and tried our luck for a while. There were a bunch of us. It wasn't long before we caught one. Well, we started hauling it in. We hauled and we hauled. We were all pulling on it. We hauled, we hauled in a big part of it. Well, we walked pulling on it for a quarter of a mile!"

I said, "Wow, wow, come on! You're exaggerating!"

And he said, "I took the axe and we cut it. There was enough for the whole bunch of us for supper. We cut the eel in two and let the other part go! We just took what we hauled in. There was enough of the eel for the whole bunch of us for supper."[11]

One joke usually tends to trigger another one, setting off a chain reaction. As the storyteller relates one anecdote, others suddenly spring to mind. When Delphine was telling the story about the eel fishermen, she thought of another fish story that she said took place in Wellington. The story has been collected elsewhere, including the United States.

— The Lantern That Was Still Lit (Le fanal allumé) —

It's like the other stories. Two men were out trout fishing. One said to the other, "I caught a big one once." And he showed how long it was, well, it was three feet long.

"Oh! come on, you're exaggerating," the other said.

"No! No! No! It's true. It's the honest truth."

"Ah," he said, not wanting to believe him. "Shorten the fish!"

"No! No! No! It's true. It was two, three feet long."

"A trout? Well, I was fishing once," the guy said, "and I caught something funny, too. I pulled and I pulled. It wasn't long before it came up. It was

Keith MacDonald's lantern from Wellington. And it was still lit!"

"Right!" he said. "He lost his lantern two years ago! And it was still lit?"

"Well," the guy said, "take a couple of feet off your trout, and I'll blow out the lantern!"[12]

Stanley Arsenault (1915–1991)

Stanley Arsenault from Summerside had a solid reputation on Prince Edward Island as a masterful teller of anecdotes. He was particularly appreciated as master of ceremonies for variety shows, banquets, and other public events, because he could entertain audiences with all kinds of stories and anecdotes that he incorporated skilfully into his introductions. Whether it was at a club or

at meetings, people would automatically gather around Stanley, so as not to miss any of his amusing stories.

Son of Philippe Arsenault and Marguerite Gallant, Stanley was born on August 6, 1915, in St. Chrysostome.[13] He obtained his teacher's licence from Prince of Wales College in Charlottetown, then taught for three years in the little schools in his parish before leaving the Island to enrol in the air force at the beginning of the Second World War. When he retired from the Canadian Armed Forces in 1965, he returned to the Island and worked as an electrical inspector in Summerside.

Stanley Arsenault had a wealth of anecdotes from which he could choose, depending on the context and the audience. He knew countless

Stanley Arsenault in 1982 (photo by Georges Arsenault)

jokes, numerous stories about the older members of the parish, and other personal incidents that he had heard about or that he himself had been involved in. To maximize the impact of his stories, he would often adapt them to suit the people who were listening to him. By changing the names of the characters, he could pretend that a particular adventure had actually happened to an individual whom everyone in the audience knew.

Speaking slowly and weighing every word, Stanley had a masterful command of the art of storytelling. Like traditional storytellers, he knew how to make his characters talk, even if it was just an amusing incident about an old man in the area.

— Old Jos Cormier (Le vieux Jos Cormier) —

It was old Jos Cormier, Jos's grandfather. He was a well-digger. One day, he decided to dig a well for himself. It was quite a distance from the house.

So he went off to dig. In those days, you did it with a pick and a shovel. When you started, the hole was eight feet wide, but it went down like a cone. That was the only way you could do it.

And so, when he got to the tip of the cone, at about 20 or 30 feet, he hit water. It was exactly 12 o'clock. "I've got to go for dinner," he thought to himself.

So he went home. He said to his old woman, "I hit water. The only thing I have left to do now is to line it with rocks to make a really nice well."

He had his dinner. Feeling cheery after his dinner, he went back to his well. But wouldn't you know it, all the earth had caved in. It was all filled up again.

"Damn," he said, "I'm going to have to dig it again!"

So he took off his cap. The shovel was sticking up out of the ground, so he put his cap on the end of the handle. Then he took his pick. After the first swing of his pick he felt discouraged. "The hell with it! I'm going over to little Félix à Hubert's place, I'll play crib with him."

It wasn't far, so off he went to play crib for the afternoon. But he didn't tell his wife. He was discouraged about the well.

Two or three men, who were hanging around together, said, "Let's go see how Jos Cormier's getting along with his well."

When they arrived, they saw all the earth, the well filled in, and the shovel sticking out of the ground with Jos Cormier's cap on it. "Jos Cormier's buried," they thought!

They went to his house and calmly told his wife. Then they went back home to get their shovels and began to dig. They dug and they dug. The old woman put on her black dress and cried. The men dug out the whole well, but they didn't find Jos. Soon they hit water. The well was all cleaned out.

Suddenly Jos Cormier arrived home. He'd beaten Félix à Hubert at three games of crib! He'd won three games of crib! When he walked into the house, his old woman nearly fainted. She thought he was buried in the well!

That happened on McIsaac Road.[14]

Like elsewhere, the tradition of storytelling in the Acadian community of Prince Edward Island was hard hit by the technological inventions of the 20th century. "Everything disappeared with radio and then television," stated Marcel Perry. "In the old days," as Lazarette Gaudet added, "it was all you had to pass the time." Julienne Pitre from Tignish Shore regretted the passing of an era when the slow pace of life lent itself to this type of entertainment, "I really loved hearing long stories like that. Nowadays, they don't exist anymore, there's nothing left but dirty jokes. That's all you hear!"

Of course, that does not mean that people do not appreciate good stories anymore. We can be entertained by stories even more than ever, thanks to television, videos, movies, radio, theatre, and even books. For those of us who lead a hectic life, these stories — be they romantic, supernatural, or full of adventures — offer moments of escape.

The traditional storyteller lost his audience long ago, but the oral tradition of the story has not totally disappeared from Acadian villages on Prince Edward Island. Although limited to jokes and anecdotes, the tradition is still alive and well. Both men and women enjoy telling these types of short tales. Go to a gathering of friends or relatives, sit in a coffee shop, or walk into the local bar and you are likely to overhear a spontaneous exchange of jokes and anecdotes told by talented storytellers.

Children still love stories, as witnessed by the impressive number of storybooks available nowadays. Traditional fairytales such as *The Three Little Pigs*, *Cinderella*, and *Little Red Ridinghood* are still favourites. All children love having stories read or told to them. I doubt, however, that they would find a story like the one our mother used to tell us whenever she wanted to end her session of storytelling:

> There was once a man and a woman who just had one child. His name was Ti-Jack. If they'd had more children, my story would have been longer![15]

Notes

[1] [Antoinette Gallant], "Rustico: on raconte," *La Voix acadienne*, 14 July 1976, p. 8. See also: Antoinette Gallant, *Little Jack an' de Tax-Man*, Bedeque, Elaine Harrison & Associates. This is a collection of the stories and anecdotes Gallant learned from her mother.

[2] Ozélie Boisvert, *Souvenirs d'enfance sur l'Île: réponse à Christian*, pp. 44–45. The text was written in 1986. Centre de recherches acadiennes de l'Île-Prince-Édouard, Fonds 76.

[3] Georges Arsenault Collection, Centre d'études acadiennes, Université de Moncton, Recording 1038, 7 August 1975. *The Magic Mill*, Type 565, according to the classification of Antti Aarne and Stith Thompson, *The Types of the Folktale*, Helsinki, Academia Scientiarum Fennica, 1961.

[4] Georges Arsenault Collection, CEA, Recording No. 1035, 7 August 1975. Type 921 — *The King and the Peasant's Son*.

[5] Luc Lacourcière, Archives de folklore, Université Laval, Recording No. 3606, 12 August 1958. Types 1641 — *The Doctor Know-All*. For another Acadian version of this story, *Le jonc volé*, see Georges Arsenault, *Par un dimanche au soir: Léah Maddix, chanteuse et conteuse acadienne*, Moncton, Éditions d'Acadie, 1993, p. 163.

[6] Georges Arsenault, *Par un dimanche au soir: Léah Maddix, chanteuse et conteuse acadienne*, op. cit., pp. 127–169.

[7] Georges Arsenault Collection, CEA, Recording No. 447, 27 June 1973. Type 402 — *The Mouse (Cat, Frog, etc.) as Bride*.

[8] In 1940, Emily Arsenault married Léo Blacquiere from Summerside. They had three children.

[9] Georges Arsenault Collection, CEA, Recording No. 666, 5 January 1973. Type 56B — *The Fox Persuades the Magpies into Bringing their Young into his House* and type 41 — *The Wolf Overeats in the Cellar*. For another Acadian version of this story, see Georges Arsenault, *Par un dimanche au soir: Léah Maddix, chanteuse et conteuse acadienne*, op. cit., pp. 134–137.

[10] In 1934, Delphine Arsenault married Aquilin Arsenault. They had thirteen children, two of whom died when they were infants.

[11] Georges Arsenault Collection, CEA, Recording No. 1064, 8 August 1975. Type 1960B — *The Great Fish*.

[12] Georges Arsenault Collection, CEA, Recording No. 1065, 8 August, 1975. Type 1920H — *Will Blow out Lantern*.

[13] In 1945, Stanley Arsenault married Lucie Arsenault from Urbainville. They had seven children.

[14] Georges Arsenault Collection, CEA, Recording No. 1238, 23 November 1976.

[15] Type 2271 — *Mock Stories for Children*.

Chapter 2
Legends

"Il m'a
conté ça pour
une vérité."

Chapter 2 — Legends

"Il m'a conté ça pour une vérité."
"He told me it was the honest truth."

It would appear that, in the course of his endless travels, the Wandering Jew skated on Prince Edward Island. At least, that is what old Sam Gallant told his grandson, Arcade S. Arsenault (1894–1982) from Abrams Village, many years ago. He said he saw him skating one starry night and that every time he tried to get closer, the elusive visitor would take off with a stroke of a skate. Old Sam claimed that he followed this mysterious individual for a long time but he was never able to catch up with him.[1]

The Wandering Jew, a legendary figure condemned to wander till the end of time because he insulted Christ on the way to the Crucifixion, was one of many individuals who once inhabited the Acadians' imaginary world. Oral tradition has preserved innumerable tales and legends about goblins, ghosts, witches, hidden treasures, haunted houses, and, of course, the always indomitable devil.

Whereas folktales are fictitious, legends are usually set in a specific place and relate to events that are believed to have happened. In many cases, the person who tells the legend is able to identify the people involved and indicate approximately where and when the events occurred. Legends and folktales have different purposes. Whereas folktales are essentially designed to entertain, legends explain supernatural phenomena and are often moralistic.

The legend does not really have any specific structure, at least nothing like that of the folktale. It can be told as a series of interconnected elements or it can appear in a conversation during which different people contribute information, ask for details, or make comments. The following story about a treasure thought to be buried in Brae came up in a conversation I had in 1974 with Agnès and Willie Arsenault from St. Gilbert:

> **Georges:** Were there any treasures buried around here?
> **Agnès:** Yes, there was one in Brae, I think. The sons of my uncle André à l'Amable tried to find it. They said they could feel it, but it kept disappearing.
> **Georges:** Who buried the treasure?
> **Agnès:** It was brought by boats, schooners that came around there.
> **Willie:** They dug everywhere in one part of Brae. I went there myself. They dug holes all over the place. I didn't find anything, of course. They thought they could feel something.
> **Agnès:** They said they could feel something, but when they got

closer it disappeared.

Willie: They likely hit a rock.[2]

Legends generally have a local flavour and relate to familiar people and places. In some cases, the history of the founding of a village or an institution involves a legend. For example, I collected the following story of a biblical nature from Madame Lucille Arsenault (1892–1996), who had heard it from a neighbour who died in 1923:

> The Old Sailor [Joseph (à Cyrille) Gallant] told us that when his grandfather came to Egmont Bay around 1812, he landed with his family along the shore by the church. They had nothing to eat but clams and quahaugs and the fish they could catch. He said there was a sort of manna that appeared on the ground in the mornings and that, in order to gather it, you had to get up really early before the sun melted it. He told us that many times.[3]

Legend has it that the apparition of a nun dressed in the habit of the Congregation of Notre Dame motivated the parishioners of Rustico to build a convent, despite the fact that they were very poor. Over the years, the nun appeared many times on the lot designated for the construction. According to witnesses, the woman, whether she was walking or sitting, always appeared preoccupied.[4] The convent was opened in 1882.

Some supernatural beings in Acadian legends, such as *lutins* (goblins) and *feux-follets* (will-o'-the-wisps), were already part of the imaginary world of their ancestors who left France to settle on this side of the Atlantic. Although they deserted Prince Edward Island a long time ago, *lutins* were the little creatures who frequented stables. At night they would carefully braid the manes of horses to make stirrups. Then they would mount the horses and ride them to exhaustion. Frank F. Arsenault (1898–1993) from Urbainville remembered that his neighbour, old Prospère Arsenault, believed in these mysterious creatures. Whenever he found his horse covered in sweat in the morning, he said he had to feed it extra grain because the *lutins* had ridden it all night.[5] Some people were convinced that these little beings were actually capable of making horses fly!

The little balls of light that can be seen moving about at night, especially in marshes and cemeteries, were referred to as *feux follets* by older people. Some said they were souls from purgatory in need of prayers,[6] while others believed that a *feu follet* was a spirit that had left someone's body temporarily, usually the body of a man of questionable morals. Island Acadians have been known to say that they have seen *feux follets* come out of people's mouths and fly into the air, leaving the people in question lying on the ground as if they were dead. Apparently, if you blocked the person's mouth, he or she would die because it prevented the *feu follet* from getting back into the body.

Although the devil appears in a great many French Canadian tales, he does not seem to have occupied a prominent position in Acadian legends on the Island. He was seen mainly by men who played cards for money, a practice condemned by the Church. On some occasions the devil would appear in the form of a black dog and sneak up on the gamblers. On others he would be disguised as a passionate card-player, but some physical feature would eventually betray his true identity.

When she was little, Marie-Anne Gallant (1886–1981) from Cape Egmont heard that the devil turned up at a card game somewhere on the western end of the Island. Apparently a stranger entered a house where a group of Protestants were playing cards for money. They soon noticed that he had horse's hooves! Panic-stricken, the men abandoned their game and huddled in a corner of the room. The devil, on the other hand, remained seated and continued playing by himself. One of the men ran upstairs to find the maid of the house and said, "You're Catholic, can't you get rid of the devil?" She grabbed her bottle of holy water, hurried downstairs, and sprinkled some holy water on the men and then on the hoofed visitor. Needless to say, the devil took off immediately![7] As a rule, the only trace the devil ever left behind was the imprint of his hand on the door or the wall of the room he had been in.

As was the case in most cultures, ghosts were also part of traditional Acadian culture. The dead came back to earth to ask for prayers, to fulfil a promise, to punish a guilty person, or for some other reason. A long time ago in Rustico, François Lebrun (c.1770–c.1814) encountered the ghost of a woman. People from the area often used to tell this intriguing story. Jérôme A. Gallant, a teacher, related it to Professor J. Henri Blanchard in 1931.

> Another legend relates that a man by the name of François Lebrun, who was coming home one evening at dusk, saw a woman walking in front of him. He thought it was Nostrice, so he called out her name, asking her to wait for him. The person who replied said her name wasn't Nostrice, but Marie Gallant (who'd been dead for some time). So her soul could rest in peace, she asked him if he would be kind enough to recite in church the seven penitential psalms every Sunday after Mass during Lent, and, if he couldn't recite them for that long, to ask Jean Doucet to finish them. According to hearsay at the time, François Lebrun recited them for a certain period, but he died and Jean Doucet finished them.[8]

Not only are legends less structured than folktales, but several people can participate in the narration. A good storyteller, however, is capable of weaving the elements of a legend so that it sounds like a real folktale. Although many storytellers also included legends in their repertoire, there were also people who specialized in legends. They told them with such conviction that one could easily be persuaded into thinking they were true stories. To give credence to the events they related, they would name familiar and reliable individuals who might have been witnesses. On occasion, they even went so far as to say that they themselves had witnessed the event. To reinforce their credibility, they would also punctuate their stories with expressions like "the story was often told to me," "so and so told it to me," or "he told me it was the honest truth."

Nellie Luttrell (1909–1993)

Nellie Luttrell, a well-known businesswoman, was one of those people who had the gift of making outlandish stories sound plausible.[9] She was born on September 13, 1909, in the parish of Palmer Road where she spent her entire life. When she was about 16 years old, her adoptive father, Captain John Perry (Poirier), opened a store in the village of St. Louis. From that time onwards, Nellie worked for the family business, which she took over in 1946 when her father died.

Nellie and her first husand, George Maillet, around 1950
(Helen Perry Collection)

In those days, the country store was a favourite meeting place for men. They could catch up on all the local gossip and reminisce about the past. During her many years behind the counter, Nellie Luttrell must have heard countless anecdotes, and her own talent as a storyteller was no doubt appreciated by her clients. A charming and intelligent woman, she was also very good at tracing people's family trees.

Like many people in the area, Nellie had her own version of the story about the haunted house, located a few kilometres from her store in a little Acadian and Irish fishing village. The events took place around 1930. This haunted house obviously made a deep impression on the people of the time, since one can still hear stories about it today in the neighbouring villages.

—The Haunted House (La maison hantée) —

You've probably heard about Pierre Poirier's house?[10]

Pierre Poirier was married to a girl called Marie Bernard. I think they had five children. Well, Pierre's wife died when the children were little. He couldn't live alone. So, after a few months, he found himself another woman. She was a Doucette, her name was Émilie Doucette. She lived on Harper Road. She was an old maid who'd never had anything to do with children. She didn't know what it was to love a child. She hadn't had children herself.

After she was married, she had her first child. Well, she liked that child, but she didn't like Pierre's children. She was pretty nasty to one of his girls. One day, she pushed her down the stairs and she broke her arm. "If you tell your father, I'll spank you," she said. "You're not to say a word about it."

The poor child was only seven or eight. She was so scared, she wouldn't have told her father for the world. Her armbone never set and an infection developed and she died from it. The stepmother wasn't any kinder to the poor girl, even when she was sick. Well, anyway, she died.

After she was dead, they'd hear someone walking upstairs, then they'd hear someone coming down the steps, coming downstairs. They'd always leave the house, because the woman was scared when she heard the noise.

One night, when they were in bed, Pierre told her she was just imagining things. She said to him, "No, you heard it yourself, you know."

Anyway, not long after they were in bed, they heard the noise out in the hall — their bedroom door was closed. They heard something walking in the hall, coming towards their bedroom. Then it knocked on the door. Pierre jumped out of bed and opened the door, but there was nothing there.

The next day, a man by the name of Arsène Poirier came to the house. You've heard of Arsène Poirier from Miscouche, haven't you? He was a travelling salesman and Pierre Poirier had a store. He arrived there at suppertime. Pierre said to him, "You might as well have a cup of tea with us." Arsène had heard about the trouble they were having, but he didn't dare ask if it was true.

They were in the middle of supper when all of a sudden they heard a sound upstairs like a pile of glass falling. Oh! there was big crash and a commotion. It made the plates rattle on the table. It was awful. At that point she said, "Ah! there's the noise we hear all the time."

Well, Arsène said, "Is that true? Is that true, is that it?"

"Yes," she replied. "I can't stay here at all, at all. As soon as I'm by myself, it torments me. It comes down the stairs and goes back up again."

The priest had said to them, "If you have the house blessed, perhaps..."

So they had the house blessed. After that, there were sounds of chains rattling under the house. They heard chains, big chains that made a racket and shook everything... Well, they said, "We don't know what we're going to do with this house, we can't stay here any longer."

Suddenly the house caught fire and burned. Then they built a new house, and after that they never heard anything. They built their new house in the same place as the old one but they never heard anything in that house.

Everybody said it was because that woman had been so nasty to the little girl and that it was the girl who was after her.[11]

Nellie Luttrell did not believe all the supernatural stories she knew. She was, however, convinced of the truth of the vision her first husband, George Maillet (1893–1956), had when he was a young man working in lumbercamps on the mainland.

— A Vision (Une vision) —

This is something my husband, my first husband, George, told me. It was true. He saw it himself. He was in the lumbercamps over in New Brunswick and he had no way of coming back. That was before I married him.

There was a guy from Bouctouche who was there. One night, they started talking about girls they'd known and gone out with. Then this man from Bouctouche said to George, he said, "I've got the most beautiful girl who ever walked on this earth. I wish you could see her, she's so beautiful."

George said, "Well, when we get out of the woods, perhaps I'll take a swing around to Bouctouche, then I'll see her."

The guy said to him, "If you want to see her tonight, I can get her to come here."

George was kind of scared, so he said, "Ah no! Don't do that."

"Yes, yes," he said, "I can get her to come here."

They were not very far from a little river and he said, "Come with me to the river and I'll get her to come."

It was around 11 o'clock at night. George was kind of scared. It kind of frightened him! But he went along anyway. Then the guy said to him, "Now, watch out, she's going to come."

A few minutes later, he saw her coming across the water. She was coming as if she had something under her feet and was just floating on top of the water. Well, she came quite close to the edge of the river. She was dressed in a long nightgown and her hair was hanging down. In those days, women wore their hair tied up on top of their head. But her hair was hanging down.

George said she was beautiful. She was blond and she was really beautiful. And there she was, standing not far from the edge of the river. Then the guy said, "That's my girl and I'm going to marry her when I leave the woods." He said the reason she was wearing a nightdress was because she was in bed asleep. He said, "I got her to come here."

Well, George saw her himself. It's not just something that this person or that person told me! George told me it was the honest truth, he saw her himself, with his own eyes. After that, he said he was kind of scared of being around that man because he thought he was kind of a sorcerer, you know! Well, he was kind of scared. He didn't stay long after that, he came back home.[12]

Like many people of her generation, Nellie Luttrell knew stories about Old Dollar. She was the best-known sorcerer in the area around Tignish and Palmer Road, and was famous for casting spells. In fact, the most popular legends among the Acadians of Prince Edward Island were the ones about sorcerers or *jeteux de sorts*, as they were usually called. In most cases, they were transients or people who had just arrived in the community, in other words individuals who could easily raise suspicions in any close-knit village where everyone knew everyone else. Mi'kmaq, who passed through at least once a year selling baskets, were thought to be able to cast spells. They were not the only ones, however. In his history of Cascumpec, Gilbert Buote states that the first schoolmaster, a Frenchman from Brittany by the name of Dominique Auffrey, was suspected of witchcraft.

> Since he could read and write, Auffrey passed as learned and of-
> fered his services as a teacher. But he didn't stay long. He conduct-
> ed himself in such a way as to raise suspicions and soon, because of
> his bizarre behaviour, people began to call him *Sorcier*. He was the
> source of so much gossip that eventually he was forced to leave the
> area.[13]

Sometimes the witch was of Acadian origin, and a well-established member of the community like Old Dollar from the Tignish area. Baptized Marguerite Dollar (1818–c.1877) and Acadian on her mother's side, she married an Acadian by the name of Michel Maillet in 1838. She was still considered an outsider because she had arrived in the Tignish area around 1832 with her father, Pierre Dollar, a schoolmaster whose origins are unknown.[14] Nothing has been transmitted by oral tradition with regard to this teacher who lived on the Island for about 12 years. In Bouctouche, New Brunswick, on the other hand, where he lived from 1845 to his death in 1855, he was reported to be one of the most famous sorcerers in the county. As Lauraine Léger points out in her book, *Les sanctions populaires en Acadie*, there are countless legends about him:

> First of all, it would appear that he was so vicious that he would balk at nothing. He had signed over the souls of seven of his descendants to the devil in order to obtain his power. He had put a hex on his own daughter because she had drawn attention to one of his secret powers. He had cast spells on people without their knowledge and then passed himself off as a doctor to cure them and be paid for his services. [...] Apparently, priests and missionaries tried everything to bring him back to a better disposition. But he always said that no priest would get the better of him and that, in any case, the devil was just as good as God.[15]

With a father that well-known, it is easy to understand how Old Dollar could acquire a reputation that even today provides a source of gossip.

— Old Dollar (La Vieille Dollar) —

There was an old woman who came from Bouctouche, New Brunswick. Her last name was Dollar. People used to call her *la Vieille Dollar*. She came here, then she married a Bernard. I think that was his name. They say she could cast spells. She had a daughter who was awfully beautiful. There was a fellow whom she wanted to come and see her daughter. She was always saying to the fellow, "Come see my daughter, come see my daughter, she's so beautiful, she'd make a lovely wife for you."

But he didn't like her. He'd say, "No." Then he said, "No. Well, I'll go a few times anyway."

But he didn't go.

So Old Dollar went to this young man's parents' home. They were young, but their son was old enough to go and see girls. They had younger children and a little baby still in the cradle. So the old woman talked and talked for a while.

The baby was healthy, he'd never been sick. After the old woman left, the child took sick during the night. Well, I tell you, he was pretty sick. In those days, it wasn't easy to get a doctor. There weren't any doctors!

Well, they took care of it, they gave it medicine, but they didn't know what was wrong with the child. All it did was cry.

That went on for two or three days. The child was almost dead. The man said to his wife, "Do you think the old woman who came here the other day cast a spell on our child because our oldest son doesn't want to see her daughter?"

"Well, it could be," she said.

So she closed all the windows tight, then the doors, then she took the child's nightshirt and put it in the oven to warm it up.

Something happened, I don't know what, but she must have forgotten it because the nightshirt caught fire. Soon they saw the old woman's husband coming. He knocked on the door, then he said, "For the love of God, take out whatever you've got in the oven! My wife's dying, she's covered in big blisters."

She was burning just like the child's nightshirt in the oven. Then they said, "Yes, yes, we'll take it out."

"She put a spell on your child," he said. "She told me she would remove the spell."

They took the shirt out of the oven, but it was too late. When he got back home, his wife was dead.[16]

According to oral tradition, the baby in question was John Arsenault, son of Léon Arsenault and Odile Doucet, who was born in 1877 in Palmer Road parish. There is no record of the old woman's death, but she must have died around that time because her husband, a widower, married the widow Geneviève Arsenault in the church at Tignish on October 8, 1878.

Emmanuel Gaudet in 1983
(Rina Martin Collection)

Emmanuel Gaudet (1910–1983)

Emmanuel Gaudet, from Harper Road, was born on November 9, 1910. Being from Palmer Road parish, like Nellie Luttrell, he also knew several stories about Old Dollar. Obviously, he never met her since she lived long before his time. However, he knew her daughter whom, as he put it, he had "hauled into the ground," in other words driven the hearse to her burial.

Like most boys of his generation, Emmanuel Gaudet[17] left school at the age of 14 or 15. When he was a young man, he worked during the winters as a lumberjack in

New Brunswick, Nova Scotia, and New Hampshire. On the Island, in addition to carpentry and running a small farm, he also worked as a fisherman's helper and a farm labourer.

Emmanuel Gaudet was an interesting and very sociable person. He liked visiting his neighbours who, in turn, enjoyed his company because he not only brought them the news, but he also told them ghost stories, a genre in which he excelled. As a little girl, Eileen Chaisson-Pendergast was impressed by this legend-teller who visited her family almost on a daily basis:

> My sister and I would sit on the oven door of the wood stove, back
> to back. And we'd listen to those terrible stories about people who
> had been turned into bulls, about horses that had been bewitched,
> and the like... We believed every word he said. We were scared to
> go to bed. In those days, we didn't have electricity, so it was just oil
> lamps. We'd take one upstairs with us to get a bit of light before
> we crawled under the covers, we were so scared.[18]

Eileen often asked Emmanuel Gaudet if he was frightened to go back home alone in the dark. His answer was always the same: "My dear child, it's not the dead who scare me, it's the living."

The following story, about Old Dollar and her daughter, is one of the many tales in this masterful storyteller's repertoire.

—The Rooster (Le coq)—

I never knew Old Dollar, myself. She was an old woman who came from Bouctouche. In those days there were people in Bouctouche and around here who could put curses on you. I can't tell you what the two of them had, but they were always doing things. Old Dollar had a daughter who got married here in Deblois, on the other road. She was almost the same as her mother, she played nasty tricks on a lot of people.

I remember once, she came over to our place. My dear mother had a bunch of chickens. At that time, we were living in Deblois, I was just a young fellow. Whenever Old Dollar's daughter saw something she liked, she had to have it. Do you know what I mean?

But my dear mother had a nice bunch of chickens and a beautiful rooster. Oh! he was a big rooster. Old Dollar's daughter came over one day and saw the rooster. She said to my dear mother, "You should give me your rooster."

"Oh," said my mother, "I can't give you my rooster."

Well, she tried coaxing my mother. But my mother said to her, "No, I'm not giving you my rooster."

With that, she left. A little while later, my mother went outside and found the rooster dead.[19]

Emmanuel Gaudet was unaware of the fact that the Dollar family had lived in West Prince before they settled in Bouctouche. As previously mentioned, Marguerite Dollar (Old Dollar) married Michel Maillet on the Island in 1838. The couple moved to Bouctouche around 1846 and then came back to settle on the Island around 1858. According to Emmanuel Gaudet, the mother used her witchcraft to a much greater extent than her daughter.

– Old Dollar Turns into an Animal (La Vieille Dollar en animal) –

When I was working in the woods near Moncton, I worked with some guys from Bouctouche. In those days, like me, they'd heard about Old Dollar. Their fathers knew all about her. She was nasty, really nasty. I never saw her, I never knew her. But I knew her daughter. Oh yes, I knew her well. It was me who drove the hearse when she was buried.

There was a man who lived near us, he was one of our neighbours for a long time. He's dead now. Old Dollar had daughters and he was seeing one of them. Do you understand? I don't know what happened between them, but he left her and started seeing another girl who lived in St. Louis. He'd go there on foot along the railway tracks.

One night he was coming home. After he'd been walking for a bit on the railway tracks, he noticed that there was a big animal following him. He said to himself, "Damn! What can that be?" He went over to the edge of the tracks, picked up a big stick and then started hitting the animal. But it didn't run away. It followed him to Deblois, right up until he turned off onto the road to Peterville. Then the animal disappeared.

It was around then that Old Dollar was crippled, I don't know for how long.

She'd gone after him, she turned herself into an animal. Yes, old John à Léon told us that. You heard him yourself, didn't you? [Emmanuel Gaudet is speaking to his wife, Marie-Blanche.] For a month or more, the old woman couldn't move, he'd pounded her so hard with the stick.[20]

Like all good legend-tellers, Emmanuel Gaudet knew stories about hidden treasures, so typical of the lore of most islands. Many people were totally convinced that Captain Kidd and other pirates had buried their treasures on the shores of Prince Edward Island. Gaudet told the following story about a treasure buried near North Cape where there had been numerous shipwrecks, no doubt caused by the long narrow reef that had formed where the waters of the Gulf of St. Lawrence and the Northumberland Strait meet. The lighthouse that overlooks the cape today was built in 1866.

— Hidden Treasures at North Cape (Les trésors cachés au cap Nord) —

Old Jérôme used to tell us years ago that in those days there was no light at North Cape. There was a huge, deadly reef with no light and no buoy.

In those days there were a lot of boats that came from France and England. When they arrived they didn't know the area very well. There was nothing to warn them to stay away from the shore. So they often landed on the reefs. There were no banks in those days. They took all their money with them, then they hid it underground. That was their bank, in those days.

People said there was a lot of money hidden around North Cape, in the spot they called the Mash. An old man by the name of Jérôme had rods, something they called "mineral rods" [divining rods]. They were made from hazelnut. You'd take a forked stick if you wanted to find water. It could find water anywhere.

Well, those fellows had one of those. I saw old Jérôme with one of them myself. They put what they called "quick silver" on the end of it. They put it on the end of the stick so they could find money, or anything, wherever it was. I mean, hard money, not paper money. Gold or silver coins, they could find them anywhere.

Well, old Jérôme fished in those days. One evening, some fellows asked him to see if he could go dig for some money with them. So he said, "All right, I'll go."

He had his rod. So one evening they took off. They didn't go in the daytime, it had to be at night. In any case, when they got there, old Jérôme said to the other fellow who was with him, "When we start digging, after we've found the spot, don't say a word. If you say anything, it'll all disappear."

"All right." They went out and they worked for a while. By God, if he didn't find a spot! His rod showed it to him. Well, he said to the other fellow, "We've got to dig here."

Well, they started digging. And they dug. Things were going well, they didn't say a word. It was dark. It was in the fall of the year. After a while, they hit something, like a pot or some other thing. The fellow yelled, "Look, look what's coming ashore!" And whatever he'd hit disappeared.

There was a big ship headed towards the shore. In those days, they called them bricks. They had a lot of sails. It was a big ship close to the shore. He said, "It was just as well we left anyway, there was nothing there anymore."

Old Jérôme had a crowbar. When the other fellow spoke, it broke a piece off the end of his crowbar.

A year or two later, he said to himself, "Ah, I think I should go back."

So he had another crowbar made and had a cross put on it near the end.

He went back one evening with another fellow. The same thing happened. The same thing happened. When they hit the spot where the pot was, the fellow yelled out that there was a big ship headed towards the shore. He had spoken. Old Jérôme said, "It broke my crowbar again, just below the cross. The cross was left on it. After that, I never went back. There was no point in going back."[21]

Old Jérôme was certainly not the only one to go looking for the elusive treasure in North Cape, as the following comment written in 1906 by the editor of the Tignish newspaper *L'Impartial* would suggest: "There is no treasure in North Cape, because a huge stretch of land has been dug over by gold diggers spurred on by imaginary dreams." The editor concluded with a moralistic remark, typical of Acadian nationalists of that period, "There are treasures on our beautiful Island, but it was not Captain Kidd, the famous pirate, who put them there. It was Providence. God asks only for strong arms to plough the earth where thousands will grow in the form of grains and vegetables."[22]

According to oral tradition, a treasure was unearthed, not in North Cape, but about 12 miles from there, in a place called Frog Pond in the village of Skinners Pond. However, as Emmanuel Gaudet relates, it was not the locals who profited from this supposed treasure, but perfect strangers.

— A Treasure Found in Frog Pond (Un trésor trouvé à Frog Pond) —

Oh yes, treasures have been found here, too. Oh yes, treasures have been found here, too. But not by people from around here. There was a house in the place called Frog Pond. Suddenly strangers arrived and asked the owners if they would rent them their house for a night. The owners had to leave the house for the night. They didn't know what to do. The strangers said to them, "We'll pay you a fair price. We guarantee we won't do any damage to your house. We won't damage anything."

So the owners said, "All right." They left the house in the evening and the people stayed there. The next morning, when the owners came back, the strangers were gone. There was nothing broken in the house. When they went down into the cellar, they found a big hole dug in the ground.

Georges Arsenault: They thought there was a treasure there?

Yes. They thought there was something there. The people knew it was there. Yes.[23]

Benoît DesRoches (1904–1989)

There was another treasure, supposedly somewhere around Miscouche, which appears to have attracted many people. It was not buried by some foreign pirate, but by the murderer Xavier Gallant (c. 1760–1813), who lived on Lot 16 in the Malpeque Bay area. Benoît DesRoches knew the story.

Benoît DesRoches was a teacher who had obtained his First Class Teacher's Licence at Prince of Wales College in Charlottetown in 1924. Very knowledgeable about the history of his parish, he also remembered information that had been passed on to him about this Acadian criminal and his treasure.[24]

Born on September 2, 1902, he was the son of William DesRoches and Obéline Aucoin. He grew up in a household where many stories were told about Xavier Gallant and the olden days. Since the DesRoches family lived near the parish church, in the wintertime their friends and relatives from the nearby villages would often stop in to get warmed up and to leave their horses in the stables before going to Sunday Mass. "They would arrive two hours before Mass," explained Benoît. "At that time, we were just young fellows and we'd listen to them. They'd be there, men and women, talking about the olden days. They told stories. I don't know how many times I heard the story about Xavier."

Benoît DesRoches in 1978 (photo by Lawrence McLagan, courtesy of the Prince Edward Island Museum and Heritage Foundation)

The sad tale of Xavier Gallant left a deep impression on the Acadian community in the early part of the 19th century. Over the years, his story gradually took on legendary proportions. In reality, it was the first documented murder in the Acadian community of Prince Edward Island. In a fit of madness, on

June 11, 1812, Xavier Gallant cut his wife Madeleine's throat in the woods near their farm. Her body was found a few days later with the help of the demented husband who was arrested and taken into custody in Charlottetown. After a short trial, he was found guilty and condemned to be hanged. However, there was a stay of execution due to questions regarding the legality of the process by which he had been convicted. Incarcerated in a filthy cell, Xavier Gallant died on November 6, 1813, before the case was settled.[25]

Several years before the crime, Xavier, or "Pinquin" as he was called, had received a sum of several hundred dollars which, at that time, represented a considerable amount of money. He received the money from a man by the name of Marsh, probably the merchant Thomas Marsh. According to witnesses at the trial, poor Xavier went mad after he became rich. It would appear that he showed signs of paranoia. He accused his wife and children of stealing his money, he thought his dog had cast a spell on him, he was convinced that his house was going to be seized, and sometimes even thought his wife Madeleine was the wife of one of his sons.[26]

As Benoît DesRoches related in 1975, Xavier Gallant obviously hid his money very well since no one has found it yet, despite numerous attempts.

— Old Xavier's Treasure (Le trésor du vieux Xavier) —

He was an old sailor who went to sea. Somehow, he obtained a treasure, at least that's what his neighbours and people who knew him called it. He was married and had children and buried his treasure in Miscouche. I can show you the place where they dug for the treasure, about 60 years later. It's not far from here, it's not even a quarter of a mile.

He went to look at his treasure and became kind of suspicious of his wife. He thought she knew where it was. He went crazy and killed her. He took her out in the woods, killed her, and then buried her. He covered her with leaves.

It wasn't long before people noticed that his wife had disappeared. After they found her body, they went looking for him. He had run off into the woods to hide.

He was like a ghost. Whenever someone saw him in one place, people would go looking for him, but he'd disappear. So they went to the priest and got him to say a Mass to find him because everybody was scared. (There weren't many people in Miscouche in those days.) They went into the woods the next day and they found him. They captured him.

After that, people started digging for his treasure. There were two women and their brother. One was Mrs. Gilbert DesRoches, her name was

Sophique or Sophie, and her sister's name was Césarine. Their brother was Manuel, I think. They went digging. I haven't been there for years, but 40 or 50 years afterwards, the holes were still there. My father and other people told me that was where they dug for old Xavier's treasure.

There were four or five holes, I can't remember exactly, but when they reached the road here, across from Midwest Sales and Services, they started digging close to the fence. They hit a big rock, so they decided to get someone the next day to move the rock. The next day they went back, but the rock had disappeared. So they continued digging. In the evening, a big dog appeared and went around the hole they'd dug, barking. He barked and barked and barked. They were scared. "This place is possessed. The devil's around here somewhere," they said. "That's enough digging."

So they left the hole and they never went back there. But someone went and filled in the hole because it was dangerous. The treasure was never found. They say there was a treasure because he had travelled a lot. They say it's gold coins from France.[27]

Since Xavier Gallant had eight children, seven of whom were alive in 1812, he has many direct descendants living today, mainly in the Evangeline Region, and around Rustico where his children settled. Even today, there are still rumours about the murderer and his treasure. The pathetic story of Xavier Gallant has been kept alive, thanks to a well-known ballad that folklorists have collected in all three Maritime Provinces, on the Magdalen Islands, in the Gaspé Peninsula, and on the North Shore of Quebec.[28] In some versions of the ballad, reference is made to the sad fate of Xavier when he was in prison:

> After several long years, news came
> That the poor criminal was to be hanged.
> He spent so long in the cruel prisons
> That worms and lice ate all but his bones.[29]

Clothilde Arsenault (1896–1985)

The Acadians from Malpeque Bay, where Xavier Gallant and his family lived, were the first to settle and clear the land around Tignish. The migration started

Clothilde Arsenault in 1982
(Judy Roach Collection)

in 1799 and included families bearing the names Poirier, Chaisson (or Chiasson), Bernard, Gaudet, Doucette, DesRoches, Arsenault, and Richard. It was not until about 1811 that the first Irish families moved into the area. From that point on, the Acadians shared the western end of the Island with these new immigrants. The two communities got along relatively well and have intermarried for several generations. Not surprisingly, however, in the early days, the Acadians were somewhat suspicious of these foreigners whose language and culture were different. Legend has it that some Irish women possessed magic powers that enabled them to cast spells. According to Clothilde Arsenault from Ascension, there was a legend in her family about an old woman by the name of Foster.

Daughter of Avis Arsenault and Marguerite Gaudet, Clothilde Arsenault was born on July 1, 1896. She was quite well-known among the Acadians of Prince County because she had lived in several different villages during her 33 years as schoolteacher. She never married and lived most of her life with her brother Émile in the family home, after their parents died. Clothilde loved to read and was familiar with the history of the Acadians and the history of her parish. She also knew many stories of the oral tradition.

— Old Mrs. Foster (La vieille Foster) —

She wasn't an Indian woman, she was an old Irish woman, old Mrs. Foster. She'd been over at Jean Gaudet's. Someone had given her some potatoes, but they couldn't deliver them, so she went over to Jean Gaudet to see if he could deliver them to her. But it was the busy season and maybe he was a person who didn't like to go out of his way for other people. In any case, he didn't go. When she left his place, she said to him, "One day, you'll do like me. You'll walk."

He had two horses. One of them, a mare, was bewitched. She would climb up into the hayloft. That happened near my grandfather's place. My mother told us about it many times. The mare would climb up into the hayloft and do all kinds of things like that. Jean Gaudet's wife and daughters were so frightened, they didn't want to sleep in the house anymore.

So Jean Gaudet went to see Father Dougald and told him about it. Father Dougald laughed at him. He didn't want to believe it. Well, Jean Gaudet said to him, "I'm going home and I'm going to kill the mare."

Then Father Dougald said, "Don't do that. I'll go myself." So he got ready, harnessed his horse, and went over there. He took his prayer book with him. I think it was the exorcisms that he read that made the mare return to her normal thin self, two or three days later. Not long after that, she died. Then Jean Gaudet had another fine young horse and it died, too. So Jean Gaudet was just like old Mrs. Foster, he had to walk.[30]

The people best-known in the province for casting spells were the Mi'kmaq or the *Sauvages*, as they were commonly called in French. Ignored by public authorities and considered by white people to be intruders, even though they had inhabited the Island for thousands of years, the Mi'kmaq were reduced to abject poverty.[31] In order to survive, they travelled from village to village, in some cases begging, but more often selling baskets, which they wove with great skill and artistry from black ash. Many people were convinced that the Mi'kmaq possessed a special power that enabled them to cast evil spells on anyone who showed the least bit of hostility towards them. Clothilde Arsenault said that her own grandparents were subjected to a punishment of this kind.

— Maple Sugar (Le suere d'érable) —

The Indians went to my grandfather Gaudet's place, too. I don't know if they were men or women. Anyway, they wanted some maple sugar. It was towards the end of winter, just before sugaring off, and my grandparents only had a little bit left. My grandparents and my old great-grandfather Sosime and his wife all lived there. In those days there were no stores, if you needed to buy sugar. In any case, they didn't give them any maple sugar.

Then they made their sugar. They made maple sugar every spring. They had a maple grove and they made maple sugar every spring. That spring, they made their sugar and their syrup as usual. When they opened up a sugar loaf, it was beautiful thick sugar all round, but in the middle it was full of ants. The same thing for the syrup. When they opened a bottle of syrup, it looked good from the outside and from the bottom, but it was the same thing, it was full of ants. So they cut down the maple trees and never made maple sugar again.[32]

Rita Perry (born in 1920)

Rita Perry (Poirier) from Tignish remembers the days when the Mi'kmaq would go through the village selling their baskets or begging. When she was young,

there were Mi'kmaq who had built a little cabin on the edge of the woods where they made their baskets. It was located in Palmer Road, not far from the house of John Perry and Marie Richard, her parents. Many people were frightened of the Mi'kmaq, so they avoided them. "Nobody bothered them. They didn't steal anything. I was never aware that those Indians stole anything, like whites might have, you know."

Born on November 28, 1920, Rita Perry was a talented storyteller who grew up in a large family.[33] Rita said that her father, who liked to tell all kinds of stories, was rather superstitious. She remembers her mother as a kind person who regularly offered her services as midwife to women in the community.

Rita Perry in 1997
(Georges Arsenault Collection)

Rita Perry recalls the fascinating stories that her parents told, especially the ones about Joe Labobe, an elderly Mi'kmaq blind man who was often in the area.

– The Beautiful Woman is Punished (La belle femme punie) –

Well, my mother told me she had a relative in Harper Road who was a beautiful woman. She was Camille's mother and was a Richard. Her father was related to my mother on my grandfather's side.

Anyway, the woman was really beautiful. She made fun of people, imitating their gestures. One day, she had scrubbed the floor and was going to throw the water outside. Just as she was throwing the water out, the old Indian came around the corner. Didn't she throw all the water on him! She laughed, of course. And he was mad! He didn't come in, he turned around. They say he did things like this [gesturing with his hands] beside the house. Then he went to the neighbour's house and told her what the woman had done. He said to her, "She laughed. She'll be blind when she dies. She'll be like me!"

And, sure enough, not long afterwards, the woman started going blind.

My mother swore to us, because she used to go and see her, that when she went to see her before she died, the woman was blind and she looked like old Joe Labobe.

Now is it a true story? My mother didn't tell lies. Maybe it was only something she imagined because she knew what the old Indian had said.[34]

Rita Perry was puzzled by that story. Her mother told her that the skin of the dying woman had turned completely yellow. Rita wondered if the woman had cancer of the liver. "Today," she added, "we have all kinds of explanations for these things. But in those days, they didn't."

Contrary to many of her contemporaries, Rita Perry's mother was not the least bit afraid of Mi'kmaq visitors, whom she received into her home and fed without hesitation. She consulted them for cures because their healing skills were well-recognized. In fact, historians question whether the early French settlers would have been able to survive if the indigenous people had not shared their knowledge of medicinal plants. Native healers were also very familiar with magico-symbolic medecine. Rita Perry thinks that she herself was cured of asthma, thanks to the Mi'kmaq healer, Joe Labobe.

— A Cure for Asthma (Une guérison de la courte-haleine) —

An Indian came to the house once. I had asthma when I was a child, and I was having an attack when he came to the house. It was old Joe Labobe. My mother said to him, "You wouldn't have any idea what I could give that child to stop her asthma, would you?"

"Yes," he replied.

"What should I do?"

"Stand her up," he said, "then make a hole in the wall. It has to be the same height or a little higher than her. Cut off a lock of hair, put it in the hole, then plug the hole. When she's grown past the hole, it'll go away."

The next day, my father took me outside, made me stand against a tree, and then made a hole. After a year, I wasn't cured. After two years, I grew past the hole.

Old Joe Labobe came to the house. My mother muttered to him, "What you said didn't happen. You told me something that wasn't true."

"Where did you make the hole?" he asked her.

"In a tree, outside."

"That's no good," he said. "The tree grows, the girl grows! Make it in the house somewhere, or on a post outside. Something that doesn't grow."

Well, they did it. I was cured of my asthma. I don't know if that's what cured me... I've never had it since then.[35]

Ozélie Boisvert (1913–2002)

Ozélie Boisvert, from Dieppe, New Brunswick, spent the first nine years of her life on the Island in the village of St. Edward.[36] Born on January 6, 1913, she was the daughter of Joseph Bernard and Sara Boisvert. Ozélie remembers very clearly Mi'kmaq men and women going from house to house, laden with baskets

Ozélie Boisvert in 1998
(photo by Georges Arsenault)

of all kinds that they would sell for between 10 and 25 cents apiece. Sometimes they would ask for a place to sleep. Ozélie's mother was kind-hearted and never refused to lodge them if her husband was home, although she was afraid of the evil spells they could cast. She would offer these passers-by pillows and covers so they could sleep beside the stove.[37]

As a child, Ozélie Boisvert was deeply marked by beliefs and superstitions: "Our lives were interwoven with strict religious practices, ghosts, and superstitions. I never heard my father talk about superstitions, but my mother had a whole collection of them."[38] Ozélie's mother believed that death could befall a family if you rocked an empty chair, if you walked on a little cross formed by wood shavings, or if you counted the buggies behind a hearse at a funeral.

The Bernard family was struck mercilessly in the fall of 1918 when Jeanne and Rosalie, two of their daughters, and their son Willie all died of the Spanish flu. Rosalie had had a strange apparition in the spring, perhaps a warning that death was near. Ozélie Boisvert was only three years old at the time, but the memories of this disturbing and inexplicable event still haunt her. The ghost appeared in Lot 7, a village known today as Cape Wolfe, where her father, Joseph Bernard, was working during the winter for a Mr. MacWilliam.

The Tall Woman Dressed in White (La grande femme blanche)

It's a story that frightened us all during our childhood. We were living in Lot 7 and we were the only Catholics in that little place. The Protestants didn't want Catholics living there, so it seems. I don't know if that's true, but that's what I heard. One day my sister Rosalie, who's dead now, was looking after my youngest brother. I was being looked after by a woman in her home because Mother was sick. On that day, Mother, who was feeling better, decided to come and get me.

My sister, who's still living, was in the house, too. It was a small house and the door was really hard to open. It had made a hole in the floor because it was so hard to close. It was in the spring, and my sister, who's still living, remembers that the door opened three times and closed three times. She didn't see anything, but my sister Rosalie, who's dead now, saw a woman dressed in white come into the house. She said she felt as if a voice was saying, "Go to the door, you won't be afraid there." When she went to the door, she met a woman who brushed against her three times with her veil and moaned three times. Then the woman left and disappeared.

Rosalie said to my other sister, "Go look around the house to see if there's anyone."

Since it was spring, it was muddy outside. They didn't see any tracks in the mud. So my sister Rosalie said, "You look after my little brother and I'll go meet Mother, maybe she's not feeling well again."

Mother saw Rosalie coming, she was really pale. Mother asked her what had happened, "Did your father drown?"

We were always scared that he'd drown. My sister Rosalie said to her, "No, a woman dressed in white came into the house." And then she fainted.

My mother then went to see the priest. He told her that another young girl had seen the same thing in the same house.

We didn't sleep there that night. We got out of there and we never went back. That was the fright we had in our childhood. Whenever we talked about the woman dressed in white, we were all scared. Sometimes when we went to bed at night, there were no lights in those days, we'd come back downstairs scared to death because we thought we'd seen the woman dressed in white.

The three children, Jeanne, Rosalie, and Willie, all died the next fall. Mother used to say that the woman's moaning was a forewarning. Mother was really superstitious.

It took us a long time to get over that fear.[39]

This type of mysterious apparition, predicting an imminent death, resembles the very popular legends of forerunners, particularly common in the Irish and the Scottish communities on the Island. These harbingers of death manifested themselves in various forms, ranging from noises, voices, and lights to phantom funeral processions. Although the sight of a funeral procession often appears as a premonition of death in Celtic legends, it is not part of Acadian supernatural lore. However, like their Irish, Scottish, and English neighbours, Island Acadians have many legends related to hidden treasures, haunted houses, sorcerers, the devil, and, of course, the phantom ship of the Northumberland Strait that was seen from time to time burning off the western shore of Prince County.

Although these tales of the supernatural are always set in Prince Edward Island, they are typical of oral traditions in Western cultures.

What were people's attitudes with regard to these beliefs and superstitions? At a time when many natural phenomena had no scientific explanation, many people were firm believers in these supernatural apparitions. Given their credulous nature, children, in particular, were easily impressed. In his memoirs, the former Premier, Judge Aubin Edmond Arsenault (1870–1968), a native of Abrams Village, states that all these supernatural stories terrified him when he was young: "As a child, the maids at home used to tell us ghost stories and I became so nervous that I would not go into a vacant room at night, nor would I sleep alone."[40] Judge Arsenault was quick to add, however, that not all Acadians in those days believed the superstitions.

Over the years, beliefs changed and people became more educated and more discerning. The farmer Frank F. Arsenault (1898–1993) never actually believed in goblins or sorcerers, but he knew people who had become slaves to their beliefs. "It was pitiful," he said.

Father Jean-François Buote (1908–1988), born in North Rustico, felt that too much was made of the supernatural: "It got people upset for nothing. Older people spent their time telling stories about ghosts and that sort of thing. Well, often they frightened young people and children. In the end, when someone was brave enough to go and look, most of the time there were neither goblins nor ghosts."[41]

Sorcerers, goblins and will-o'-the-wisps have long since disappeared from the Acadian villages of Prince Edward Island. People still talk about the occasional haunted house, hidden treasure, or omen of death. In recent years, possible sightings of unidentified flying objects have become yet another rich source for new Acadian legends.

Notes

[1] Georges Arsenault Collection, Centre d'études acadiennes, Université de Moncton, Manuscript 125, 30 July 1974.

[2] Georges Arsenault Collection, CEA, Recording 688, 18 July 1974.

[3] Georges Arsenault Collection, CEA, Manuscript 212, 29 May 1974.

[4] J.-Henri Blanchard, *Une paroisse acadienne de l'Île-du-Prince-Édouard*, Rustico: J.-Henri Blanchard, 1937, pp. 49–50. The author quotes the legend told in the diary of the Rustico Convent.

[5] Georges Arsenault Collection, CEA, Manuscript 202, Frank F. Arsenault, 11 November 1976.

[6] Eunice Arsenault Collection, CEA, Manuscript 21, 1971.

[7] Georges Arsenault Collection, CEA, Manuscript 3, 1 September 1971.

[8] Prince Edward Island Public Archives, J.-Henri Blanchard Fonds, 2330, Series C-2, Letter from Jérôme A. Gallant (Collette, NB) to J.-Henri Blanchard, 30 March 1931.

[9] Nellie was married three times. Her first husband was George Maillet, her second husband was Simon Luttrell, and her third was John Monaghan. She was Nellie Luttrell when I recorded her.

[10] The names of the various members of the family in the legend are fictitious.

[11] Georges Arsenault Collection, CEA, Recording 353, 5 June 1973.

[12] Georges Arsenault Collection, CEA, Recording 352, 5 June 1973.

[13] "La Paroisse de Cascumpec," L'Impartial, March 17, 1904, p. 3. The Auffrey in question is the ancestor of all the Auffreys in southeastern New Brunswick. According to a letter, dated 21 May 1821, from Father Antoine Gagnon to Monseigneur Joseph-Octave Plessis, bishop of Quebec, this young Frenchman taught in Barachois (NB) after he left the Island. Father Gagnon states that Dominique Charles Auffrey, a goldsmith by trade, was born in Lamballe, Brittany, in 1794. He was a soldier under Bonaparte in 1813 and was dismissed in 1814. In 1816, Auffrey went to Newfoundland and, from there, he made his way to PEI where he taught school for three years. While living on the Island, he fathered a child, but refused to marry the mother. "He wanted to marry a girl other than the one with whom he sinned, feeling an aversion to her, maintaining that he did not seduce her, but was seduced by her, and that it was she who sought him out." Before leaving the Island, he gave the girl's parents "what they asked for" in the presence of a justice of the peace. Archives of the Archdiocese of Quebec, Series 311 NB C.N. 5-54.

[14] He is the ancestor of the Dallaires in southeastern New Brunswick. He signed his name Petre Daller. According to a family tradition, "he appears to have been brought up, as a young child, by a captain. He was educated and later also became a captain, but stopped sailing to become a teacher." He married Sophie Petitpas from Tracadie, Nova Scotia. See Émery LeBlanc, La vie à Sainte-Marie, 1984, pp. 15–16.

[15] Lauraine Léger, Les sanctions populaires en Acadie, Montreal: Éditions Leméac, 1978, pp. 140–142.

[16] Georges Arsenault Collection, CEA, Recording 349, 5 June 1973.

[17] In 1942, at the age of 32 years, Emmanuel Gaudet married Imelda Poirier. They had three children. She died of tuberculosis in 1947. He married Marie-Blanche Poirier in 1960.

[18] Georges Arsenault Collection, CEA, Recording 1612, 22 December 1991.

[19] Georges Arsenault Collection, CEA, Recording 1137, 10 November 1976.

[20] Georges Arsenault Collection, CEA, Recording 1137, 10 November 1976.

[21] Georges Arsenault Collection, CEA, Recording 1140, 10 November 1976.

[22] "Un trésor serait caché au 'North Cape,'" L'Impartial, 29 March 1906, p. 1.

[23] Georges Arsenault Collection, CEA, Recording 1141, 10 November 1976.

[24] Benoît DesRoches taught for several years in Acadian one-room schools and finished his career as a schoolteacher at Summerside High School. He was president of the PEI Association of Acadian Schoolteachers and one of the founding members of the Acadian Museum. He married Émilie Arsenault from Bloomfield in 1942 and Margaret MacDonald in 1979.

[25] "Xavier Gallant," *Dictionary of Canadian Biography*, Vol. V, Toronto: University of Toronto Press, pp. 335–336.

[26] Georges Arsenault, *Complaintes acadiennes de l'Île-du-Prince-Édouard*, Montreal: Éditions Leméac, 1980, pp. 136–137.

[27] Georges Arsenault Collection, CEA, Recording 1208, 31 December 1975.

[28] For a comparison of the legend and the ballad, "Le meurtrier de sa femme," see Georges Arsenault, *Complaintes acadiennes*, op. cit., pp. 117–168.

[29] Roger Matton Collection, Archives de folklore, Université Laval, Recording 186, 21 July 1958. Ballad sung by Benoni Benoît, aged 56.

[30] Georges Arsenault Collection, CEA, Recording 392, 4 June 1973. For another version of this legend, see Sister Saint-Hildebert, "La sorcellerie," *La Petite Souvenance*, No. 12 (June 1985), pp. 25–26.

[31] Alan Andrew MacEachern, "Theophilus Stewart and the Plight of the Micmacs," *The Island Magazine*, No. 28 (Fall-Winter 1990), pp. 3–11.

[32] Georges Arsenault Collection, CEA, Recording 393, 4 June 1973.

[33] In 1941, Rita Perry married Joseph Perry from Palmer Road. They had three children. In 1955, the family moved from Palmer Road to Tignish.

[34] Georges Arsenault Collection, CEA, Recording 1705, 12 November 1992.

[35] Georges Arsenault Collection, CEA, Recording 1705, 12 November 1992.

[36] Born in Rogersville, New Brunswick, she moved to St. Edward with her parents at the age of six. When she was nine, the family moved to Rumford, Maine. Ozélie completed the equivalent of her high school diploma at the convent school of the Dominican Sisters in Lewiston. In 1938, when she was visiting Rogersville, she met the teacher Alfred Boisvert, whom she married.

[37] Ozélie Boisvert, *Souvenirs d'enfance sur l'Île : réponse à Christian*, Text written in 1986, PEI Acadian Research Centre, Fonds 76, p. 49.

[38] *Ibid.*, p. 58.

[39] Georges Arsenault Collection, CEA, Recording 1497, October 1988.

[40] A. E. Arsenault, *Memoirs of the Hon. A. E. Arsenault, Former Premier and Retired Justice, Supreme Court of Prince Edward Island*, Charlottetown, 1951, p. 6.

[41] Georges Arsenault Collection, CEA, Recording 579, 21 June 1974.

Chapter 3
The Folksong Tradition in the Chaisson Family

"Ma mère chantait du matin au soir."

Chapter 3 — The Folksong Tradition in the Chaisson Family

"Ma mère chantait du matin au soir."
"My mother sang from morning till night."

> "My mother sang all the time. If she didn't sing out loud, she'd hum. We heard her singing those old songs all the time."
>
> "My father never worked without singing. Working and singing went together."

These comments by Florence Bernard (born in 1916) from Abrams Village and Marcel Perry (1914–1997) from Peterville illustrate the role that singing used to play in people's daily lives. The repertoire of the Acadian singers was composed mainly of folksongs from the Old World, but also of local compositions, literary songs, and hymns.

The folksongs referred to in this chapter are songs that originated, for the most part, in France, where they were composed several centuries ago or, in some cases, even farther back. According to specialists, many of these songs date back to the Middle Ages and are so old that all trace of their authorship has been lost. These songs from France, passed on from one generation to the next, travelled easily in time and space, so it is not surprising that they landed on the shores of Prince Edward Island.

I was amazed to discover how many French folksongs that traditional Acadian singers on the Island knew. Their repertoire included every type of song from medieval ballads to children's rhymes. A number of the singers I met were able to sing songs, such as the old ballad called *La nourrice du roi* ("The King's Nurse"), which are little known elsewhere in Canada or even in France. *La nourrice du roi* appears in the collection of traditional songs compiled in Prince Edward Island around 1905 by the parish priest in Mont Carmel, Father Pierre-Paul Arsenault, in collaboration with Father Théodore Gallant, a musician. Their collection is considered to be the first of its kind in any Acadian community in the Maritimes, the Magdalen Islands, or in the Gaspé Peninsula.

As has been the case in other Francophone communities, the number of Island Acadians capable of handing down this venerable musical tradition has declined steadily over the years. However, it is still possible to find individuals who have treasured this precious legacy inherited from their ancestors.

In 1972, I had the opportunity of listening to several of these prolific traditional singers when I met the Chaisson family from St. Edward in the parish of Palmer Road. After meeting the very likeable 82-year-old Maggie Chaisson, her daughter Marie-Anne Gallant, and her niece Denise Allain, I soon realized that I had stumbled into a veritable oasis of traditional French songs. In the years that followed, I met several other members of the family, including Maggie Chaisson's grandchildren. Thanks to the three generations of this family, I was able to record approximately 150 different songs, 13 of which are presented in this chapter.

In some ways, it is surprising that such a wealth of French oral traditions has survived in a community such as St. Edward, where English is the language spoken most fluently and, in the case of a great many of the villagers, the only language spoken. Of course, this is a relatively recent phenomenon. Founded around 1880 by Acadian families from the neighbouring parish of Tignish, St. Edward remained predominantly French-speaking until the 1960s, despite the fact that there has always been a strong Anglophone presence in both the outlying area and in the village itself where several Irish families live. Among the many factors that have contributed to the anglicization of the community, the most obvious ones are intermarriages between Francophones and Anglophones, an English-language educational system, a lack of religious services in French, and the inferior status generally attributed to the French language.

Maggie Chaisson (1890–1987)

In 1972, when I met Maggie, the oldest member of the Chaisson family, I was surprised to discover that she spoke very little English — at least not enough to conduct a conversation. Being rather shy, she felt uncomfortable with an English-speaking person, especially a stranger. When I arrived at her house, she mistook me for an Anglophone. I had hardly crossed the threshold and not even had time to say hello when she turned and whispered to her daughter, "I'm not singing for him, he's English." But she changed her mind as soon as I spoke to her (in French, of course), and as soon as she learned that my mother was a native of St. Edward.

Maggie Chaisson (née Marguerite Gaudet) had lived her whole life on the Island and most of the

Maggie Chaisson in 1980
(photo by Georges Arsenault)

time in the village of St. Edward. Born on April 10, 1890, she was the daughter of Sosime Gaudet and Blanche Bernard. At the age of 19, she married a young man from the village, Joseph Chaisson (1889–1952), and they had 10 children. Life was not easy for the Chaisson family. As one member of the family put it, "We were poor! We were as poor as could be!" While Joseph looked after their small, relatively unproductive farm, Maggie often had to leave home to earn a few dollars doing housework for families who were better off, or working as a cook in the fish plants during the lobster season. Her eldest daughter, Auldine, was forced to leave school when she was 11 years old to look after her younger brothers and sisters when her mother was out working.

No doubt songs helped Maggie through the hard times in her life. As a result, her children remember her not as a downtrodden or sad woman, but as a courageous and a very gentle person who spent her life singing. Her son Emile says, "My mother sang from morning till night. When she worked, she sang. Whether it was knitting, doing the dishes, or doing her washing by hand, she sang." Although he does not consider himself a singer, Emile knows the words of many of his mother's songs. He told me that he never made any particular effort to learn the words, but they are stored in his memory simply because he had heard them day after day. Several years after his mother died, Emile, who had lived with her for a good part of his life in the family home, decided to make a list of the songs he could remember. His list, which he told me was incomplete, contains about 220 songs. He also remembers several English songs that his mother sang.

It would appear that Maggie Chaisson inherited her talent as a singer from her mother. There were other members in the family who were also good singers, especially John Gaudet, who was the parish choirmaster for many years. According to his nephew, Alyre Chaisson, he was "the best choirmaster who ever sang there."

It is obvious that Maggie had retained many of her mother's songs and that she had enriched her own repertoire over the years by adding songs she had learned from various individuals. Maggie had a beautiful voice and older people in the village remember with nostalgia the days when it was customary to call upon her to sing at weddings. Her renditions of the many wedding songs she knew invariably brought tears to the eyes of the bride and her friends.

Even though Maggie Chaisson could play the harmonium by ear, she always sang without accompaniment, often keeping time with her foot. She always sang in a lively manner, even if the songs related sad stories, as is the case for *La belle Françoise* ("Beautiful Françoise"), in which a young girl weeps for her lover who is going off to war. This very old song, well-known in both Canada and France, is sung to numerous melodies with many different refrains. Maggie Chaisson's version is particularly noteworthy because of its simplicity.

C'est la belle Françoise, *melon lon lon,*

—La belle Françoise—

Original key: D major

C'est la bel - le Fran - çoi - se, me - lon lon

lon. C'est la be - le Fran - çoi - se qui

veut se ma - ri - er, qui veut se

ma - ri - er, qui veut se ma - ri - er !

C'est la belle Françoise, *melon lon lon,*
C'est la belle Françoise
    qui veut se marier! (*ter*)

Son amant va la voir, *melon lon lon,*
Son amant va la voir
    le soir après souper. (*ter*)

Il a trouvé Françoise, *melon lon lon,*
Il a trouvé Françoise
    sur son lit qu'elle pleurait. (*ter*)

— Oh! qu'a'-vous donc Françoise, *melon lon lon,*
Oh! qu'a-vous donc Françoise,
    qu'a'-vous à tant pleurer? (*ter*)

— J'ai bien entendu dire, *melon lon lon,*
J'ai bien entendu dire
à la guerre vous alliez. *(ter)*

— Ceux qui vous l'ont dit, belle, *melon lon lon,*
Ceux qui vous l'ont dit, belle,
ont dit la vérité. *(ter)*

Préparez mes chemises, *melon lon lon,*
Préparez mes chemises
aussi mes blancs mouchoués. *(ter)*

Vous viendrez me conduire, *melon lon lon,*
Vous viendrez me conduire
jusqu'à l'ombre du rocher. *(ter)*

Quand nous 'ons 'té en mer, *melon lon lon,*
Quand nous 'ons 'té en mer
j'l'avons entendue pleurer. *(ter)*

C'est la belle Françoise, *melon lon lon,*
C'est la belle Françoise
qui est bien désolée.[1] *(ter)*

Beautiful Françoise

Tis beautiful Françoise, *melon lon lon,*
Tis beautiful Françoise
who wants to marry! x 3

Her sweetheart goes to see her, *melon lon lon,*
Her sweetheart goes to see her
one night after supper. x 3

He found Françoise, *melon lon lon,*
He found Françoise
on her bed weeping. x 3

— Oh! what have you, Françoise, *melon lon lon,*
Oh! what have you, Françoise,
    that you weep so? x 3

— I heard it said, melon lon lon,
I heard it said
    that you are off to war. x 3

— Those who told you that, my dear, *melon lon lon,*
Those who told you that, my dear,
    told you the truth. x 3

Prepare my shirts, *melon lon lon,*
Prepare my shirts
    and my white handkerchiefs. x 3

You'll accompany me, *melon lon lon,*
You'll accompany me
    to the shade of the big rock. x 3

When we were out at sea, *melon lon lon,*
When we were out at sea
    we heard her weeping. x 3

Tis beautiful Françoise, *melon lon lon,*
Tis beautiful Françoise
    who is so heartbroken. x 3

Maggie's husband, Joseph Chaisson, also liked to sing and had a nice voice. To relax after a day's work, they would often sing duets together. Apparently they both had strong voices that carried well. In the summer, when the windows were open, their singing could be heard throughout the neighbourhood and often attracted visitors. "One night," Maggie recounted, "my late husband Joseph and I were singing. There was a fellow living on the hill, he got up in the night and came over. It was around one o'clock. He said, 'For Jesus' sake! You made me get up and come over here, your songs are so beautiful!'"

Maggie and Joseph also enjoyed singing songs they could sing as dialogues, such as the following tune, called *L'ivrogne* ("The Drunkard"), in which a husband comes home late at night, inebriated as is his wont. His wife, not the least bit pleased, is waiting, ready to scold him. This song has been collected in Canada on many occasions, especially in the Acadian areas of the Maritime Provinces, but also on the Magdalen Islands and in the Gaspé Peninsula. Conrad Laforte does not list any European version of the song in his *Catalogue de la chanson folklorique française*.

L'ivrogne

Original key: G major

Al - lons, ivrogne, sor - tir du lo - gis, Ne vois-tu pas qu'il

pas - se mi-nuit? Tu es par - ti d'em - puis ce ma - tin,

Tu dois a - voir le ven - tre bien plein. Tu es comme un homme qui n'a

pas de rai - son, Et qui veut pas res - ter à la mai - son.

— Allons, ivrogne, sortir du logis
Ne vois-tu pas qu'il passe minuit?
Tu es parti d'empuis ce matin,
Tu dois avoir le ventre bien plein.
Tu es comme un homme qui n'a pas de raison,
Et qui veut pas rester à la maison.

— Ah! Tout doux, tout doux, ma p'tite femme, tout doux,
Il ne faut pas parler si haut.
J'ai eu l'malheur de prendre un coup d'trop,
Et tout à coup je me suis senti chaud,
Alors j'attendais qu'les voisins furent couchés
Pour les empêcher de bavasser.

— Comment, ivrogne, oses-tu v'nir ici
Pour me conter de pareilles menteries?
La raison est, j'arrivai hier à soir,
Et tu croyais de m'trouver endormie.
Alors tu croyais de venir t'mettre au lit
Sans le laisser savoir à Jolie.

— Tout doux, tout doux, ne parle pas si haut,
Tu connais bien les gens d'en haut.
Tu sais qu'ils sont tous des bavards[2]
S'ils s'aperçoivent que j'arrivai tard,
Tout d'suite ils diront que j'arrivai soûl
Et qu'on s'a chicané comme des fous.

— Tout doux, tout doux, ma p'tite femme, tout doux,
Il ne faut pas parler si haut.
Oui, je savais que t'étais ben chez vous,
Et moi aussi, j'étais ben chez nous.
Tu m'as pris, je t'ai pris, tu m'as et je t'ai,
Faut mieux endurer son chien que de l'tuer!

The Drunkard

— Come, drunkard, get out of the house
Don't you see it is long past midnight?
You've been away since this morning,
Your stomach must be good and full.
You're like a man with no common sense
And who doesn't want to stay at home.

— Oh! Sweet dear, sweet dear, my little wife, sweet dear,
You must not speak so loudly.
I had the misfortune of drinking one too many,
And all of a sudden I felt drunk,
So I waited till the neighbours had gone to bed
To prevent them from gossiping.

— How dare you, drunkard, come back home
To tell me such silly lies?
The reason is I was here last night,

And you thought you would find me sound asleep.
So you thought you could slip quickly into bed
Without even waking your Jolie.

— Sweet dear, sweet dear, don't speak so loudly,
You know all too well the folks upstairs.
You know well they are all gossips
If they see that I came home late,
Right away they'll say that I am drunk
And that we've indeed fought like fools.

Oh! Sweet dear, sweet dear, my little wife, sweet dear,
Don't speak so loudly.
Yes, I know you were happy at your parents'
And I too, I was happy at home.
You took me, I took you, you have me and I have you,
Tis better to endure one's dog than to kill it![3]

Like the two previous compositions, the following song was recorded in June 1972 when Maggie Chaisson was 82 years old. Despite her age, she still sang very well, obviously taking great pleasure in sharing songs she had known virtually all her life. Sitting in her rocking chair, she would pull from her memory ballads, children's songs, and humourous songs like *Ah! venez voir, mesdames* ("Oh! Come See, My Ladies"). The internationally known Acadian singer from New Brunswick, Édith Butler, was so taken by the way Maggie interpreted this amusing song that she added it to her own repertoire and later recorded it.[4]

Ah! venez voir, Mesdames

Original key: C* major

J'ai trou - vé un gar - çon, le plus beau des garçons,

Ma mèr' qui veut l'a-voir, moi, j'vou - lais le gar - der.

Refrain

Ah ! ve - nez voir, Mes-da - mes, quoi c'que j'ai trou - vé.

Sur la gerbe⁵ de blé, devinez quoi j'ai trouvé,
J'ai trouvé un garçon, le plus beau des garçons.
Refrain : *Ah! venez voir, Mesdames,*
           Quoi c'que j'ai trouvé.

J'ai touvé un garçon, le plus beau des garçons,
Ma mère qui veut l'avoir, moi, j'voulais le garder.

Ma mère qui veut l'avoir, moi, j'voulais le garder.
Il faut aller sus l'juge pour se faire juger.

Il faut aller sus l'juge pour se faire juger.
Le juge condamne la vieille : «Tu pourrais t'en passer.»

Le juge condamne la vieille : «Tu pourrais t'en passer.»
Elle reste assez fâchée, l'embouri a séché.

Elle reste assez fâchée, l'embouri a séché.
À la place de l'embouri, une citrouille qu'a poussé.

À la place de l'embouri, une citrouille qu'a poussé.
Ç'a pris deux teams de ch'vals pour lui faire arracher.

Oh! Come See, My Ladies

Upon the sheaf of wheat, guess what I did find,
I found a handsome boy, the handsomest young boy.
Refrain: *Oh! come see, my ladies*
What I indeed did find.

I found a handsome boy, the handsomest young boy,
Mother wants to have him, but I want to keep him.

Mother wants to have him, but I want to keep him.
We're off to see the judge, for he alone will judge.

We're off to see the judge, for he alone will judge.
The judge says to the crone, "You can do without him."

The judge says to the crone, "You can do without him."
So angered she did stay, her belly-button dried.

So angered she did stay, her belly-button dried.
From her belly-button, the biggest pumpkin grew,

From her belly-button, the biggest pumpkin grew,
It took two teams of horses, to pull it out of her.[6]

Normally we associate lullabies with gentle, soothing tunes designed to lull
a baby to sleep. The lullaby called *Dors, dors, dors* ("Sleep, Sleep, Sleep") would
probably have just the opposite effect, judging from the way it was sung to me by
Maggie Chaisson and her niece Denise Allain. They sang it together at a lively
tempo. The words of this intriguing and little-known Acadian lullaby resemble
some of the lines in the following lullaby from the former French province of
Poitou:

> Fais dodo, petiot, dodo!
> Ta m'man est à la rivière
> En train d'laver tes drapiaux [langes]!
> Fais dodo, dodo,
> A t'apport'r un gros tété
> Grous, bin grous,
> Comme la tête à not' chin Mouré![7]

Go to sleep, little one, to sleep!
Your mummy is down at the river
Busy washing your nappies [diapers]!
Go to sleep, to sleep,
She'll come with a big tit to suckle
Big, big, as big
As our dog Mouré's head!

Dors, dors, dors

Original key: F# major

Dors, dors, dors, Ma pe - tite à la que-dor.   Ta

mèr' qu'va au ruis-seau   Pour la - ver tes dra-peaux.

Tiens- toi pa-rée,   Quand j'ar-riv'rai,   La soupe est sur la tabl'   Pa-

rée à man - ger.   Dors, dors, dors,   Pe-tite à la que-

dor,   Ta mère est au ruis- seau   Pour la- ver tes dra-peaux.

Dors, dors, dors,
Ma petite à la queue d'or.
Ta mère qui va au ruisseau
Pour laver tes drapeaux.
Tiens-toi parée,
Quand j'arriv'rai,
La soupe est sur la table
Parée à manger.
Dors, dors, dors,
Petite à la queue d'or,
Ta mère est au ruisseau
Pour laver tes drapeaux.

Sleep, Sleep, Sleep

Sleep, sleep, sleep,
My sweet little goldilocks.
Mother's at the river
Busy washing diapers
Be ready for me
When I come back,
The soup's on the table
All ready to eat.
Sleep, sleep, sleep,
My sweet little goldilocks,
Mother's at the river
Busy washing diapers.[8]

Alyre Chaisson (1911–1993)

Of all the boys in the Chaisson family, it was the eldest son Alyre who really kept his parents' musical traditions alive. Born on January 2, 1911, he lived in St. Edward until the age of 50, when he moved with his family to Summerside, about 100 kilometres from the village where he grew up. When he was living in St. Edward, Alyre owned an acre of land and kept a cow, a horse, several pigs, and some chickens. He did various things to earn a living. He was hired as a fisherman's helper, worked in lobster plants, and spent several winters in lumbercamps in New Brunswick. After he moved, he was a gravedigger, and then worked for the municipality of Summerside. Alyre was a talented craftsman who had learned from his father-in-law how to make woven baskets from black ash like the Mi'kmaq. In fact, he was able to earn a bit of money by selling his baskets, especially the ones used for potato-picking.

Like his mother, Alyre had what appeared to be an inexhaustible repertoire of songs. Most of them came from his parents, but he had also learned some from his grandparents, particularly his maternal grandmother, Blanche Gaudet. When he was a child, his paternal grandfather, John Chaisson, taught him *Dans la prison de Londres* or *Le prisonnier de Nantes* ("In the London Prison" or "The Prison of Nantes"). It would appear that it was the only song his grandfather ever sang. Over the years, Alyre expanded his repertoire with songs he learned from other singers, although he did not recall having picked up any in the lumbercamps where he spent several winters.

Sarah and Alyre Chaisson in 1992 (photo by Georges Arsenault)

In 1932, he married a neighbour, Sarah Gaudet (born in 1912), and they had 13 children. Just as his parents had done, Alyre used to sing duets with his wife, who had a beautiful rich voice. Sarah's father, Jérôme Gaudet, sang in the church choir. Sarah had been a choir member at the church in Palmer Road and later in Borden where she had lived for several years. Obviously her husband taught her songs, but she also learned many from other members of the Chaisson family, whom she had known since her childhood. Sarah told me that she often went over to help Alyre's older sister, Auldine, take care of the younger children when Maggie was working outside the home. "We'd sing and we'd look after the children," she said.

Alyre Chaisson knew a wide variety of songs, including numerous ballads. The following ballad, which he sang with his wife, tells the tragic story of a woman who suffered the abuse of her husband for a long time before she was finally saved and avenged by her brother. It is a very old ballad that has often been collected in both France and Canada.

L'y a sept ans

Original key: G major

L'y a sept ans que je suis ma - ri - é(e)

J'ai pas eu d'joie que la pre - mièr' jour - née.

J'ai pas eu d'joie que la pre - mièr' jour - née.

L'y a sept ans que je suis marié(e), (*bis*)
J'ai pas eu d'joie que la première journée. (*bis*)

Le lendemain, ma mie, creusez un puits. (*bis*)
Dans ce puits-là, trois petits rasoués il y a. (*bis*)

Le plus petit m'a percé les côtés (*bis*)
Et le plus grand m'en a fait tout autant. (*bis*)

Je lui demande pour aller me promener. (*bis*)
Vas-y[9] putain mais n'y sois[10] pas longtemps. (*bis*)

J'ai 'té trois jours avant de m'en revenir (*bis*)
— Oh! qu'as-tu fait, qu'as-tu fait si longtemps? (*bis*)

J'ai vu trente-et-un cavaliers, (*bis*)
C'est dans la bande mon frère Olivier était. (*bis*)

— S'il te demande où sont toutes tes couleurs, (*bis*)
Tu lui diras, oh! malade que t'as 'té. (*bis*)

S'il te demande où sont toutes tes servantes, (*bis*)
Tu lui diras, à la cour du roi. (*bis*)

S'il te demande où sont tous tes p'tits enfants, (bis)
Tu lui diras, en paradis ils sont. (bis)

S'il te demande où ton mari a 'té, (*bis*)
Tu lui diras, en promenade il est. (*bis*)

— Bonjour mon frère, que l'bonjour te soit donné. (*bis*)
— Bonjour ma soeur, que l'bonjour te soit donné. (*bis*)

Il lui demande : « Où sont toutes tes couleurs? » (*bis*)
Tout haut a' y dit : « Oh! malade que j'ai 'té. »
Tout bas a' y dit : « Malmenée que j'ai 'té. »

Il lui demande : « Où sont toutes tes servantes? » (*bis*)
Tout haut a' y dit : « À la cour du roi. »
Tout bas a' y dit : « Oh! j'en ai jamais eu. »

Il lui demande : « Où sont toutes tes enfants? » (bis)
Tout haut a' y dit : « En paradis ils sont. »
Tout bas a' y dit : « Oh! il les a tous tués. »

Il lui demande : « Où-c'ton mari a 'té? (bis)
Tout haut a' y dit : « En promenade il est. »
Tout bas a' y dit : « Caché au pied de mon lit. »

Prend les escaliers et il monte au grenier. (bis)
— Bonjour beau-frère, que l'bonjour te soit donné.
Pris son épée et au coeur lui a planté.

Seven Long Years

For seven long years a wife I've been,   x 2
I've had no joy save for the first day.   x 2

The very next day, my love, dig a well.   x 2
In that well, three razors lay.   x 2

The smallest razor my ribs did pierce   x 2
The biggest razor hurt me just as much.   x 2

I asked him if I could go visiting.   x 2
— Go, you tart, but don't be long.   x 2

Three days went by before I returned.   x 2
— What did you do, what did you do for so long?   x 2

— I saw one and thirty horsemen coming,   x 2
'Twas in the band my brother Olivier rode.   x 2

— If he asks you where all your colour's gone,   x 2
You'll tell him how terribly sick you've been.   x 2

— If he asks you where all your servants have gone,   x 2
You'll tell him, they've all gone to the king's court.   x 2

If he asks you where all your children are,   x 2
You'll tell him, they're all in paradise.   x 2

If he asks you where your husband has gone,   x 2
You'll tell him, my husband has gone a-walking.   x 2

— Good day, my brother, may the day be good.   x 2
— Good day, my sister, may the day be good.   x 2

He asks her, "Where has all your colour gone?"   x 2
Loudly, she says to him, "Oh! sick I've been."
Softly, she says to him, "Ill-treated I've been."

He asks her, "Where have all your servants gone?"   x 2
Loudly, she says to him, "They're at the king's court."
Softly, she says to him, "I've never had one."

He asks her, "Where have all your children gone?"   x 2
Loudly, she says to him, "They're in paradise."
Softly, she says to him, "He's killed them all."

He asks her, "Then where has your husband gone?"   x 2
Loudly, she says to him, "My husband's gone a-walking."
Softly, she says to him, "Hiding at the foot of my bed."

He heads for the steps and goes right upstairs.   x 2
— Good day, brother-'n-law, may the day be good.
He takes his sword and plants it in his heart.[11]

In 1981, the first time I recorded him, Alyre Chaisson was 70 years old. He was retired and living alone with his wife Sarah. With a lot of spare time on his hands, he would often sing to fill the emptiness of the house. He said to me, "Sometimes I find myself alone when my wife is gone to prayer meetings, I'd be all alone, so I sit in my rocking chair and sing."

Alyre would often sing with his eyes closed, so he could concentrate better and remember the words. He knew all his songs by heart, but sometimes he had to dig deep into his memory if he had not sung some of them for many years.

One of Alyre Chaisson's favorite songs is called *Christophe* ("Christopher"). Many versions of this amusing song have been found in both Canada and France. It relates the story of a husband who goes to market to sell the family chest, knowing that his wife's lover, the village miller, is hidden inside!

Christophe

Original key: C major

Chris-tophe qui s'en va - t-au mar-ché C'é -
tait pour vendre et pour ach'-ter. Il a pas pu tout
mar-chan-der son beurre et son fro-ma - ge. Il s'en retourne à
la mai-son, oh! quel tris-te voy-a-ge.

Christophe qui s'en va-t-au marché
C'était pour vendre et pour acheter.
Il a pas pu tout marchander
    son beurre et son fromage.
Il s'en retourne à la maison,
    oh! quel triste voyage.

Sa femme le voit venir de loin
A' pleure de peine et de chagrin.
Oh! al' a dit : "Meunier, va-t-en,
    car je vois v'nir Christophe.
J'ai une trop grand' peur qu'il te voira,
    oh! cache-toi dans mon coffre."

Christophe, i' dit, tout en rentrant :
— Ma femme, i' fait un gros mauvais temps.
Dans le pays où je deviens
    où j'ai eu aucune offre,
Si nous voulons manger du pain,
    faudra vendre le coffre.

— Ah! taise-toi, pauvre mari,
Tu parles comme un homme pas d'esprit.
Tu vendras tes beaux habits
    et moi, mes belles robes
Et nous ferons autant d'argent
    et laisse-moi donc mon coffre.

Le p'tit est dans l'berceau
S'écrie : "Papa, l'meunier est d'dans!"
— Taise-toi, taise-toi, petit enfant,
    dis-en plus davantage,
C'est aujourd'hui je vends l'oiseau,
    je le vends dans la cage.

Christophe, i' retourne au marché
Encore de quoi à marchander.
Oh! j'en demande oh! cinq cents francs
    il est bon et valable,
Je ne sais pas quoi c'i' y a dedans
    ça pèse, c'est comme le diable.

Ah! c'est vous autres, mes jeunes gens
Quand vous irez voir vos catins,
Quand vous irez voir vos catins
    rentrez pas sus Christophe
Car qu'i' vous fera comme moi,
    i' vous vendra dans l'coffre.

Christopher

Christopher goes off to market
He wanted to sell and to buy.
But he couldn't bargain all
    his butter and his cheese
So he went back home
    oh! what a sad voyage.

His wife saw him coming from afar
She weeps with sorrow and chagrin
Oh! she says, "Miller, go home,
    because I see Christopher coming.
I'm too afraid that he will see you,
    oh! hide in my chest."

Christopher says as soon as he enters,
— My good wife, the weather is very bad.
In the country from whence I come
    I had not a single offer
If we want to eat bread,
    we have to sell the chest.

Oh! hush, hush, my poor husband dear,
You're like a feeble-minded fool.
You'll sell your most beautiful suits
    and I, my most beautiful dresses
And we'll make just as much money
    so leave me my chest.

The little child lying in his cradle
Cried, "Papa, the miller's in the chest!"
— Hush, hush, little child,

say not another word,
For today I'll sell the bird
    I'll sell him in his cage.

Christopher went back to market
With more to bargain for.
— Oh! I want but five hundred francs for it
    it's good and valuable,
I don't know what there is inside
    it's as heavy as the devil.

Ah! for all you other young men
When you go visiting your mistress,
When you go visiting your mistress,
    don't go to Christopher's
Because he'll do with you what he did to me
    he'll sell you in the chest.[12]

As already noted with regard to *La belle Françoise*, the theme of the soldier or the sailor who has to leave his wife or sweetheart to go off to war is not uncommon in the traditional French song. Alyre Chaisson was particularly fond of this genre, which he referred to as "war songs." The following example, *Je me suis marié le vingt-cinq de septembre* ("I Married on the Twenty-Fifth of September"), is found throughout Canada and is a special favourite of traditional Acadian singers. It is interesting to note, however, that in his *Catalogue de la chanson folklorique française*, Conrad Laforte does not indicate that any versions of this song were found in France. Alyre and his wife Sarah sang it as a duet when I recorded it in 1993.

Je me suis marié le vingt-cinq de septembre

Original key: E♭ major

Je me suis ma-ri - é le vingt - cinq de sep -
tem - bre Qui s'trou-vait le lun - di. Le mar - di
faut par - tir. J'ai eu un com - man - de -
ment Pour al - ler prendr' les ar - mes. Pour
al - ler prendr' les armes, M'en al - ler au com - bat.

Je me suis marié le vingt-cinq de septembre
    Qui s'trouvait le lundi.
    Le mardi faut partir.
J'ai eu un commandement pour aller prendr' les armes.
    Pour aller prendr' les armes,
    M'en aller au combat.

Le jour de mon départ, le monde versait des larmes,
    Père et mère et frères et soeurs,
    Ils versiont tous des pleurs.
J'ai pris mon blanc mouchoir pour essuyer mes larmes,
    En essuyant nos deux yeux
    Foullit se dire adieu.

Je me suis marié, j'en ai du regret dans l'âme
    Ah! la femme que j'ai pris
    Elle me cause de l'ennui.
J'avais pourtant marié une si jolie p'tite femme
    C'était une fille d'honneur
    Elle a eu du malheur.

À vous autres mes jeunes garçons, sur moi prenez exemple
    Ne vous mariez donc pas
    Tant qu'la guerre durera.
Car dans le mariage on a du doux plaisir(e),
    J'estimerais bien mieux mourir
    Que de me voir partir.

Qui c'qu'a fait la chanson? C'est moi sous les feuillages,
    À l'ombrage d'un ormeau,
    Au chant des p'tits oiseaux.
Oiseau, oui, sur la branche il vole, se jette en l'air(e)
    Si j'voltigeais comme lui,
    J'irais voir ma chérie.

I Married on the Twenty-Fifth of September

I married on the twenty-fifth of September
    And that was on a Monday.
    Tuesday I had to leave.
I received an order to take up arms.
    To go to take up arms,
    To war I had to go.

The day of my departure, everyone did weep,
Father, mother, brothers, sisters
    They all shed tears.
I took my white handkerchief to wipe my tears,
    Wiping our eyes
    We said our good-byes.

I married and I regretted it in my heart
    Oh! the wife I took,
    She causes me such pain

Yet I married such a beautiful little woman
　　She was an honourable girl
　　She had a misfortune.

To you other young boys, take my example
　　Don't get married then
　　As long as there's war.
Because in marriage there's such sweet pleasure,
　　I would much prefer to die
　　Than to have to leave.

Who composed this song? It's me under the branches
　　In the shade of an elm tree
　　To the songs of little birds.
Yes, the bird on the branch can fly, take off into the air
　　If I took flight with him
　　I would see my darling.[13]

Marie-Anne Gallant (born in 1915)

The most beautiful voice in the Chaisson family is unquestionably that of Marie-Anne, Maggie and Joseph's second daughter, born on September 7, 1915. Like her mother, Marie-Anne spent her whole life in St. Edward where she married Joseph B. Gallant in 1936. They had 11 children and lived in a small house next door to Marie-Anne's parents. It was from her mother, with whom she was very close, that Marie-Anne learned most of the songs in her repertoire.

As a young woman, Marie-Anne worked in the local lobster canneries, and as a maid in several households, where she remembers learning a number of songs. Like her mother, she enjoyed singing while she did her housework, especially when she was doing the dishes.

Since she was very generous with her time, I was able to record her singing on several occasions between 1972 and 1993. The accuracy of her memory was truly impressive. She appeared to remember the words of many songs without any difficulty whatsoever, an indication that they were still part of a tradition that was very much alive. She would start by singing the tune, then the words would come automatically.

Marie-Anne Gallant in 1992
(photo by Georges Arsenault)

Like her mother and her brother, Marie-Anne knew many songs that seem to have been forgotten by other traditional singers on the Island. One of these is called *La courte paille* ("Drawing Straws"). The version she sang was quite different from the one we learned in school that began *"Il était un petit navire qui n'avait ja, ja, jamais navigué"* (There once was a little boat that ne-, ne-, never sailed). The prominent Canadian folklorist, Marius Barbeau, wrote that this particular song "has been intimately linked to the oral traditions of French Canada from its very beginning."[14] It is also the best-known sailor's song in France. It would appear that it originated in Brittany and travelled not only to French-speaking countries, but also to Spain, Portugal, England, and Scandinavia, changing languages along the way.[15]

L'y a sept ans nous sommes en mer

Original key: B major

L'y a sept ans nous sommes en mer (e),

L'y a sept ans nous sommes en mer (e), y'a

sept ans que j'sons é - car - tés, Prenez cou -

ra - ge ! y'a sept ans que j'sons é - car -

tés, Pre - nez cou - rage, bon ma - ri - é.

L'y a sept ans nous sommes en mer, (*bis*)
     y a sept ans que j'sons écartés,
Prenez courage!
     y a sept ans que j'sons écartés,
Prenez courage, bon marié.[16]

Au bout de la septième année (*bis*)
     les vivres ah! qui nous ont manqué,
Prenez courage!
     les vivres ah! qui nous ont manqué,
Prenez courage, bon marié.

Il faut tirer la courte paille (*bis*)
     de qui de nous sera mangé,
Prenez courage!
     De qui de nous sera mangé,
Prenez courage, bon marié.

La plus courte arrivit au maître, (*bis*)
     s'a-t-écrié : « Grand Dieu, pitié! »
Prenez courage!
     s'a-t-écrié : « Grand Dieu, pitié! »
Prenez courage, bon marié.

Mon petit mousse, mon petit mousse, (*bis*)
     veux-tu donner ta vie pour moi?
Prenez courage!
     veux-tu donner ta vie pour moi?
Prenez courage, bon marié.

Il faut que je monte dans ces mâts, (*bis*)
     je vois la terre de tous côtés,
Prenez courage!
     je vois la terre de tous côtés,
Prenez courage, bon marié.

Je vois là-bas sur ces montagnes, (*bis*)
      les filles ah! qui se promenont,
   Prenez courage!
      les filles ah! qui se promenont,
   Prenez courage, bon marié.

Je vois là-bas c'est dans ces îles, (*bis*)
      ma mère qui nous fait à souper,
   Prenez courage!
      ma mère qui nous fait à souper,
   Prenez courage, bon marié.

Seven Years at Sea

We have been at sea for seven years,   x 2
      for seven years we've been lost,
   Oh! Take courage!
      for seven years we've been lost,
   Oh! Take courage.

At the end of the seventh year   x 2
      all our food was gone,
   Oh! Take courage!
      all our food was gone,
   Oh! Take courage, good sailor.

We will have to draw straws   x 2
      for which one of us will be eaten,
   Oh! Take courage!
      for which one of us will be eaten,
   Oh! Take courage, good sailor.

And the captain, who drew the short straw,   x 2
      cried out, "Oh Lord, have pity!"
   Oh! Take courage!
      cried out, "Oh Lord, have pity!"
   Take courage, good sailor.

My little boy, my little boy,   x 2
    will you give your life for me?
Oh! Take courage!
    will you give your life for me?
Take courage, good sailor.

I have to climb up the masts,   x 2
    I see land in all directions,
Oh! Take courage!
    I see land in all directions,
Take courage, good sailor.

Yonder on those mountains I can see   x 2
    young girls oh! out walking,
Oh! Take courage!
    young girls oh! out walking,
Take courage, good sailor.

Yonder on those islands I can see   x 2
    my mother making supper for us,
Oh! Take courage!
    my mother making supper for us,
Take courage, good sailor.[17]

The following song called *L'ermite* ("The Hermit") tells the story of a hermit who was proud of having seduced a beautiful young girl. However, his conquest soon gets the better of him and he returns to his hermitage, not only empty-handed, but impoverished. The song is of French origin, but in Canada it has only been collected in Acadian communities. It has a lovely tune which Marie-Anne Gallant sang beautifully.

Original key: F major

L'au - tre jour en m'y pro-me - nant Le long de ces p'tits bois char - mants, Dans mon che - min j'ai ren - con - tré U - ne tant jo - lie dé - moi - sel - le, Tout' à son gué.

L'autre jour en m'y promenant
Le long de ces p'tits bois charmants,
Dans mon chemin j'ai rencontré
Une tant jolie démoiselle,
Tout à son gué[18].

De là, j'ai ôté mon chapeau,
Je l'ai saluée comme il faut
En lui disant : « Y viendrez-vous
Dans ma tant jolie ermitage
Pour y faire l'amour. »

— Ah! oui, ermite, oui je irai.
Peignez, frisez-vous comme il faut.
Je prendrai mon jupon vert
Ça sera pour saluer l'ermite
Dans son désert.

Ermite, prêtez-moi de l'argent,
Je vous la rendrai le coeur content.
Il mit la main dans son gousset,
Cent écus d'or prit dans sa bourse,
Il lui mit en main.

Mais quand la belle a eu l'argent,
Elle a pensé tout autrement,
— Ermite, laissez-moi donc aller
Dans votre jardin y prendre haleine
Et je reviendrai.

Mais quand la belle a 'té dans l'jardin,
Elle a pensé tout autrement.
— Adieu, ermite, oui, je m'en vas
Comme une perdrix qui s'envole,
Avec ton argent.

Mais quand l'ermite vut qu'elle venait pas,
Il s'en retourne à son jardin.
— Adieu, Céleste, oui tu t'en vas
Comme une perdrix qui s'envole
Avec mon argent.

The Hermit

The other day while I was walking
Through these charming little woods,
Along the way, I did meet
Such a pretty young maiden,
Happy and carefree.

I doffed my hat to her,
I greeted her politely
And said to her, "Will you come with me
To my very pretty hermitage
To talk of love with me."

— Ah! yes, hermit, I will indeed.
Comb and curl your hair nicely.

I shall wear my pretty green skirt
And that will be to greet the hermit
In his desert.

Hermit, could you lend me money,
I will repay you happily.
He put his hand in his purse,
A hundred gold coins he did take,
To put into her hands.

But when the maiden had the coins,
She thought quite differently,
— Hermit, let me take a walk
In your garden for a breath of air
And I'll come back.

But when the maiden was in the garden,
She thought quite differently.
— Farewell, hermit, yes, off I go
Like a partridge who flies away,
With all your money.

When the hermit saw she wasn't back,
He went into his garden.
— Farewell, Céleste, you've gone away
Like a partridge who flies away,
With all my money.[19]

Drownings, voyages, and battles at sea are all common themes in the tradi-tional French song. There are many seafaring adventures in the Chaisson family repertoire, some of Acadian origin, while others, like the following song which Marie-Anne called *Sur l'assurance* ("On the Leeward Side"), are from France. This ballad, which describes a battle between a French vessel and a Dutch ship, is not well-known in Canada.

Sur l'assurance

Original key: B major

Sur l'as - su - ran - ce de l'î - le Blan - che,

Trois jours, trois nuits j'ons 'té mouil-ler.

Et quand ça vient sur les onze heu - res, Sur les

onze heures du mi - di, J'ons dit : A - mis, faut le-ver

l'an - cre Et aus - si bien ap-pa - reil - ler.

Sur l'assurance de l'île Blanche,
Trois jours, trois nuits j'ons 'té mouiller.
Et quand ça vient sur les onze heures,
Sur les onze heures du midi,
J'ons dit : « Amis, faut lever l'ancre
Et aussi bien appareiller. »

Et quand j'avons arrivé au large
J'ons-t-aperçu au-d'vant de nous,
J'ons-t-aperçu un gros navire
Qui porte pavillon flamand.
Nous savons pas s'il est en guerre
Ou si c'est un bâtiment marchand.

Le capitaine de ce gros navire
S'a-t'écrié d'un air guerrier :
« Amène, amène, oh! si, amène
Ta chaloupe en dehors
Que je visite dans ton navire
Et que j'te donne ton passe-pas[20].

Le capitaine de ce p'tit navire
S'a-t-écrié d'un air guerrier,
Il lui a dit : « Viens-y toi-même
Si tu veux nous visiter,
Là, tu voiras dans mon navire
Ça qu'il y a de préparé. »

La première décharge qu'on leur donne,
Ce fut soixante coups de canon.
On n'y voyait que feu, que flammes
Prendre du derrière jusqu'en avant,
Tous ces boulettes et ces gournables[21]
Nous les 'ons fait caler à fond.

On the Leeward Side

On the leeward side of White Island,
For three days and three nights we were anchored.
And when the eleventh hour came,
At eleven in the morning,
We said, "Friends, we must raise anchor
And we must set sail."

And when we reached the open sea
We saw ahead of us,
We saw a big sailing ship
It was flying the Flemish flag.
We didn't know if it was a warship
Or if it was a merchant ship.

The captain of this big sailing ship
Cried out in a war-like tone,
— Bring alongside oh! bring alongside
Your launch boat

So that I can visit your ship
And I'll give you your passport.

The captain of the little ship
Cried out in a war-like tone,
He said to him, "Come over yourself
If you want to visit us,
Then, you'll see in my ship
What we have ready for you."

The first warning that we gave them,
Was sixty cannon shots.
There was nothing but fire and flames
From bow to stern,
With all those cannon balls and grenades
We sank them to the bottom of the sea.[22]

Denise Allain (1909–1997)

During my first recording session at Maggie Chaisson's in June 1972, I met not only her daughter Marie-Anne, but also their neighbour and close relative, Denise Allain. Denise's father, Joseph Gaudet, and Maggie Chaisson were brother and sister, and her mother, Marie-Jane Chaisson, was Maggie's husband's sister. Widowed at a young age, Denise's mother later married Joseph (Jos Onézime) Arsenault.

Denise was born on March 29, 1909, in St. Edward and grew up in a musical household since her "second" father, Joe Onézime, was one of the village fiddlers and a member of the church choir. Her mother was not a singer and in fact, Denise's sister Anna Doucette said that she had never heard her mother sing a single song. Denise was very young

Denise Allain in 1993 (photo by Carrie Ann Doucette, courtesy of *West Prince Graphic*)

when she started going over to the Chaisson house on a daily basis, and it was there that she learned a good part of her extensive repertoire of songs. In 1930, she married Benoît Allain, a young widower also from St. Edward. They had nine children and lived a few houses down the road from the Chaissons'.

Denise differed from other singers, not only because of her powerful voice and nasal twang, but also because of the way she interpreted her songs. She sang ballads better and with more intensity than anyone else, stressing the plaintive and dramatic aspects. A joyful person, Denise also liked catchy tunes and generally loved music. She enjoyed playing the harmonium and the spoons. Whenever she was with friends or was at a kitchen party, people would invariably ask her to sing, something she rarely refused. According to her sister, Anna Doucette, she was not "bashful." Her children said she sang a lot in the evenings when she was knitting or sewing by the light of the oil lamp. A talented seamstress, she made all her children's clothes from second-hand clothing. She also earned a few extra dollars sewing for various people in the village.

Like Marie-Anne Gallant, Denise Allain had not forgotten the old songs since she still sang them when she was doing her housework. As a general rule, she was able to remember most of the verses. The following folksong from her repertoire, *Par un dimanche au soir* ("One Beautiful Sunday Night"), has been collected frequently in French-speaking countries. It tells the story of a young girl who rejects her boyfriend in favour of another suitor.

Par un dimanche au soir

Original key: C minor

Par un di-manche au soir-(e) En m'en allant d'veiller, J'ai ren-con-tré la bel-le,
Ell' chan-tait un' chan-son : Trans-vi-dons
les bou-teil-les, Rem - plis-sons les fla-cons.

Par un dimanche au soir(e)
En m'en allant d'veiller,
J'ai rencontré la belle,
Elle chantait une chanson :
Transvidons les bouteilles,
Remplissons les flacons.

Je me suis approché d'elle
Pour y parler d'l'amour.
Elle m'a bien dit, sévère :
— Retire-toi d'ici,
J'en ai trouvé un autre
Que j'l'aimais plus que toi.

— S'il faut que j'm'y retire,
Oui, j'me retirerai,
Dans un couvent, la belle,
J'irai finir mes jours.
Le monde pourra bien dire
Qu'y a plus d'amour pour nous.

Vivons chers camarades,
Y a plus d'amour pour nous.
Les filles sont si volages,
Nous les aimerons plus.
Quand même bien qu'elles nous aiment,
Nous autres, j'les aimerons plus.

One Beautiful Sunday Night

One beautiful Sunday night
After an evening's outing,
I met my fair maiden
Singing a song,
Let's empty the bottles,
Let's fill up the flasks.

I approached her
To speak of my love.
And angrily she said,
— Get away from me,
I have found another
Whom I love more than you.

— If I must leave you,
Yes, I will go,
To a convent, my dear,
I will go there for the rest of my life.
People will be able to say
Love has betrayed us.

Live and let live, friends,
There's no more love for us.
Maidens are so fickle
We won't love them anymore.
Even if they love us,
We won't love them anymore.[23]

À la claire fontaine ("By the Clear Spring"), like the song *La courte paille*, is one of the most popular folksongs in French Canada. There are numerous versions of this beautiful ballad that undoubtedly crossed the Atlantic with the first French settlers. One of the versions sung by the traditional singers on Prince Edward Island was hardly known at all elsewhere before Edith Butler sang it on her record *De Paquetville à Paris*. She discovered this beautiful version of *À la claire fontaine* when she heard the 1972 recording I had made of Denise Allain.[24]

À la claire fontaine

Original key: A major

À la claire fontaine, m'en allant me promener,
J'ai trouvé l'eau si belle que je me suis baigné.
Refrain : N'allez pas trop vous tra-la-la,   (ter)
        N'allez pas trop vous baigner.

J'ai trouvé l'eau si belle que je me suis baigné.
Oh! c'est au pied d'un chêne que je me suis reposé.

Oh! c'est au pied d'un chêne que je me suis reposé.
Dans la plus haute branche, le rossignol chantait.

Dans la plus haute branche, le rossignol chantait.
Chante, beau rossignol, chante, toi qui as le coeur gai.

Chante, beau rossignol, chante, toi qui as le coeur gai.
Tu as le coeur à rire, moi, je l'ai à pleurer.

Tu as le coeur à rire, moi, je l'ai à pleurer.
J'ai perdu ma maîtresse, je n'peux la retrouver.

J'ai perdu ma maîtresse, je n'peux la retrouver.
Pour un bouquet de roses que je lui ai refusé.

Pour un bouquet de roses que je lui ai refusé.
Je voudrais que la rose s'rait encore au rosier.

Je voudrais que la rose s'rait encore au rosier.
Et le rosier lui-même à la mer qui s'rait jeté.

By the Clear Spring

By the clear spring, as I was strolling along,
I found the water so beautiful that I went in for a swim.
Refrain: *Do not go tra-la-la too much,* x 3
Do not go swimming too much.

I found the water so beautiful that I went in for a swim.
By the shade of the big oak tree I laid myself down.

By the shade of the big oak tree I laid myself down.
Perched on the highest branch, the nightingale was singing.

Perched on the highest branch, the nightingale was singing.
Sing, nightingale, sing, you with a gay heart.

Sing, nightingale, sing, you with a gay heart.
You have the heart to sing but I have the heart to weep.

You have the heart to sing but I have the heart to weep.
I have lost my sweetheart and I cannot find her.

I have lost my sweetheart and I cannot find her.
For a bouquet of roses that I refused her.

For a bouquet of roses that I refused her.
Would that the rose be still on the rosebush.

Would that the rose be still on the rosebush.
And that the rosebush be tossed into the sea.[25]

James Chaisson (born in 1936)

One of Maggie Chaisson's first grandchildren, James (Jimmy) Chaisson,[26] was
born on July 20, 1936. Son of Alyre and Sarah, he grew up in St. Edward surrounded by singers, both men and women. He remembers hearing his parents
and grandmother singing quietly while they worked. In fact, that is how he
learned many of his songs.

In 1963, like his parents, he moved to Summerside. He then went to Ontario to work for
a few years. In addition to being employed as a
fisherman's helper for several fishing seasons, he
found work potato-picking. His main source
of income, however, came from basketweaving.
When he was only nine years old, his father
made him help make hundreds of potato baskets
to fill the orders from the large stores in Prince
County. Until recently, James made a variety of
black ash baskets, mainly for the tourist trade.

Of all the French songs he heard his family sing, James Chaisson said that he preferred
the ballads. The following one, entitled L'île
aux Loups, tells the story of a sailor who dies
at sea. James' parents, grandmother, and aunt

James Chaisson in 1996
(Photo Georges Arsenault)

Marie-Anne all sang it frequently. It has been collected on many occasions
in Eastern Canada, although it has not been found in France, which indicates
perhaps that it was composed on this side of the Atlantic.

L'île aux Loups

Original key: E♭ major

Quand j'ons par - ti pour l'île aux Loups, Nous croy-ions
bien c'est de nous sau - ver. Un vent du
nord s'a - t-é - le - vé, Un vent é- pou- van -
ta - ble Qui nous a bien 'té me-
nés Vingt - cinq cent milles au lar - ge.

Quand j'ons parti pour l'île aux Loups,
Nous croyions bien c'est de nous sauver.
Un vent du nord s'a-t-élevé,
Un vent épouvantable
Qui nous a bien 'té menés
Vingt-cinq cent milles au large.

Ma foi, l'y a presque vingt ans
Que je navigue sur ce bâtiment,
Oh! je croyais ni Dieu ni vent,
Ni Dieu, ni vent, ni mer(e).
À présent me voilà donc
À périr sur la mer(e).

Ma foi, l'y a presque vingt ans
J'ai pas reçu aucun sacrement.
Si j'avais pas jeté à l'eau,
À l'eau mes caspulaires,[27]
Je s'rais pas 'ci aujourd'hui
À périr sur la mer(e).

Quand je s'rai mort et enterré,
Pavillon rouge que vous metterez
Et vous chant'rez à haute voix :
« La mort d'un capitaine
Qui est mort sur ces eaux,
Sur ces eaux écumantes. »

C'est pas ma mort que je regrette,
Y en a qui la r'gretteront plus que moi.
Oh! c'est mes chers petits-t-enfants
Aussi leur tendre mère.
Les petits diront aux plus grands :
« Nous avons plus de père. »

Wolf Island

When we set sail for Wolf Island,
We thought it was to take shelter.
A north wind suddenly came up,
A terrible, terrible wind
That carried us at least
Twenty-five hundred miles off shore.

My God, it's been near twenty years
Since I have been sailing this ship,
Oh! I feared neither God, nor wind,
Neither God, nor wind, nor sea.
Now here am I
About to perish at sea.

My God, it's been near twenty years
Since I have received the sacraments.

If I'd not thrown overboard,
· Overboard my scapulars,
I would not be here today
About to perish at sea.

When I am dead and buried,
A red flag you will fly for me
And you will sing forcefully,
"The death of a good captain
Who died on these waters,
On these foaming waters."

It is not death that I regret,
Others will regret it more than me.
Oh! it is my dear little children
And their sweet mother.
The young to the old will say,
"We've lost our father."[28]

The 13 songs in this chapter constitute a representative sample of the hundreds of old French folksongs that formed the repertoire of the traditional singers from the little village of St. Edward on the western end of Prince Edward Island. These men and women also knew many Acadian songs composed locally, along with a number of French literary songs, such as *Le petit Grégoire* ("Little Gregory") and *Au Parson* ("Visiting Parson") by Théodore Botrel.

The Chaisson family's repertoire is even more impressive if one includes the large number of English-language songs they were also able to sing. In fact, all these singers knew a wide variety of English songs, some traditional, others local or literary.

It is truly wonderful to see the rich cultural heritage preserved by members of one family for such a long time. All these singers were born and brought up in the same close-knit part of the little village of St. Edward. Within this one Acadian "clan," not only are there prolific singers but also outstanding storytellers and excellent fiddlers.

Despite the fact that over the last few decades it has been difficult to maintain French as a spoken language in this part of Prince Edward Island, the musical spirit has been preserved intact by Maggie Chaisson's many descendants. Although the children of Alyre and Sarah Chaisson, of Marie-Anne Gallant, and of Denise Allain are still able to sing some of the French songs they learned from their parents, most of them prefer country and western songs in English. Their children — the fourth generation and the most affected by anglicization — know few, if any, French songs.

Maggie Chaisson regretted that young people were no longer interested in learning her songs and that they had abandoned all the old French tunes in favour of the popular hits in English that one can hear on the radio any time. Needless to day, she was pleasantly surprised in 1972 when a young 20-year-old man entered her house, not only to listen to her traditional French songs, but to record them!

Notes

[1] Georges Arsenault Collection, Centre d'études acadiennes, Université de Moncton, Recording 180, June 1972. See Conrad Laforte, *Le catalogue de la chanson folklorique française*, Quebec, Presses de l'Université Laval, 1977–1987, I.B.9, *La belle Françoise*.

[2] Maggie Chaisson says *buvards* (drinker).

[3] Georges Arsenault Collection, CEA, Recording 166, June 1972. Conrad Laforte, *op. cit.*, III.F.8, *L'ivrogne qui revient à minuit*.

[4] Édith Butler, *Édith Butler à Paquetville*, SPPS, PS-199911, 1980.

[5] Maggie Chaisson says *chapelle* (chapel).

[6] Georges Arsenault Collection, CEA, Recording 114, June 1972. Conrad Laforte, *op. cit.*, I.H.8 *L'anguille adjugée à la jeune*.

[7] Léon Pineau, *Le folklore du Poitou*, Poitiers, Le Bouquiniste (c.1892), 1977, pp. 460–461.

[8] Georges Arsenault Collection, CEA, Recording 385, 6 June 1972. This lullaby does not appear in Conrad Laforte's catalogue.

[9] Sarah and Alyre say *lui*.

[10] Sarah and Alyre say *soueille*.

[11] Georges Arsenault Collection, CEA, Recording 114, June 1972. Conrad Laforte, *op. cit.*, II.A.7, *La maumariée vengée par ses frères*. For other versions of this song, see Marius Barbeau, *Le rossignol y chante*, Ottawa, Imprimeur de la Reine, 1962, pp. 147–156.

[12] Georges Arsenault Collection, CEA, Recording 1388, 18 March 1981. Conrad Laforte, *op. cit.*, II.O.65, *Christophe*.

[13] Georges Arsenault Collection, CEA, Recording 1753, 27 May 1993. Conrad Laforte, *op. cit.*, II.H.30, *Le départ du soldat nouvellement marié*.

[14] Marius Barbeau, *En roulant ma boule*, Ottawa, Musée national de l'homme, 1982, p. 50.

[15] *Ibid.*, pp. 52–53.

[16] The word should be *marinier* (petty officer, waterman), but since it is not part of Island Acadians' vocabulary, it was replaced with *marié* (groom), which sounds similar.

[17] Georges Arsenault Collection, CEA, Recording 979, 4 August 1975. Conrad Laforte, *op. cit.*, I.B.13, *La courte paille*.

[18] The word should be *gré*.

[19] Georges Arsenault Collection, CEA, Recording 986, 4 August 1975. Conrad Laforte, *op. cit.*, II.C.25, *L'ermite joué par la belle*.

[20] This should be *passeport*.

[21] This should be *grenades*.

[22] Georges Arsenault Collection, CEA, Recording 1023, 7 August 1975. Conrad Laforte, *op. cit.*, II.A.69, *La prise du vaisseau*. Laforte includes under the same title two different songs with a similar theme.

[23] Georges Arsenault Collection, CEA, Recording 161, June 1972. Conrad Laforte, *op. cit.*, II.E.23, *Galant, retirez-vous*. Laforte groups under the same title two different songs with a similar theme. There is an Acadian variant similar to Denise Allain's song on the recording *Acadie et Québec*, RCA Victor, CGP 139.

[24] Édith Butler, *De Paquetville à Paris*, Disques Kappa, KPL-1111, 1983. Édith Butler sings the words of a more widely known version of the song, but uses the melody and the refrain from Denise Allain's version.

[25] Georges Arsenault Collection, CEA, Recording 182, June 1972. Conrad Laforte, *op. cit.*, I.G.10, *À la claire fontaine*.

[26] In 1956, James married Anna Bernard from St. Edward. They had 10 children. In 1987, he married Brigitte Gaudet (née Gallant).

[27] This should read *scapulaires* (scapulars).

[28] Georges Arsenault Collection, CEA, Recording 1750, 14 November 1992. Conrad Laforte, *op. cit.*, II.K.13, *Le naufrage en mer*.

Chapter 4
Songs Composed on the Island

"Venez entendre le récit."

Chapter 4 — Songs Composed on the Island

"Venez entendre le récit."
"Come listen to the story."

The Acadian community on Prince Edward Island has produced many folk poets who have left numerous songs describing various events pertaining to life on the Island. These local compositions are perhaps not quite as polished as the songs from France, which have been passed on by oral tradition for centuries, but they are certainly not without interest. They offer a wealth of information on the moral and social issues that interested ordinary people, such as religious beliefs, social equality, community spirit, honesty, and traditions. These songs also illustrate the important role that celebration plays in the Acadian mentality.

This authentically Acadian repertoire is comprised of a variety of songs, some recounting tragic events, others happy ones. A number of the songs are humourous and even satirical. Some of the ones that have withstood the test of time date back to the beginning of the 19th century, such as the ballad about Xavier Gallant who murdered his wife in 1812. Another ballad from the same period relates the misfortunes of a group of Acadians who, in order to escape the unreasonable demands of their landlord, left their village in the Malpeque area to settle in Egmont Bay and Mont Carmel.[1]

Unlike the traditional songs from France, these songs composed on the Island are usually not anonymous. As a rule, there are enough clues in the song to enable a listener, with a bit of research, to identify the time, the place, and even the author. Although these local songs are sometimes more than 20 verses long, they were generally composed by men and women who were either illiterate or who had very little education. Léah Maddix (1899–1986), a songmaker from Egmont Bay, could read and write, but she never actually wrote down any of her songs. It would appear that the muse visited her during her nights of insomnia:

> It is as if the song just comes to me. I compose them when I'm in bed [...] I compose them, then in the morning they're all there. No, I don't forget them... whether they have 12 verses or whatever. The next morning, I remember the song exactly as I composed it.[2]

Local songmakers did not create their own tunes. They borrowed well-known melodies that suited the rhymes and the themes of their own songs. In some cases, they kept lines from the original song and incorporated them into their composition.

It is difficult to say how many Acadian songs have actually been composed on the Island. The ones that have been collected and preserved by folklorists probably only represent a fraction of the total number. Fortunately, some of them have attracted the attention of traditional singers, so that over the years they have been transmitted from one person or one village to another. Some of these Island songs have even spread to the mainland and neighbouring islands.

Firmin Gallant

The *complainte* or ballad about the drowning of Firmin Gallant from Rustico is an example of a local song that travelled out of the area where it was composed. Collected in Prince County and in southeast New Brunswick, it forms part of the amazing repertoire of Acadian ballads composed on Prince Edward Island. By definition, a *complainte* or ballad is a mournful narrative song that commemorates a tragic event, usually a drowning, but sometimes a murder, or an accidental death on the road or at work.

Ballads are the longest form of local songs and have been composed in numerous Acadian communities throughout the Maritimes and Quebec. It is surprising, however, that some areas known for their rich oral traditions, such as Cheticamp in Cape Breton, have not produced any ballads. Prince Edward Island, on the other hand, appears to have been fertile ground for this type of oral literature. There are about 20 known ballads composed on the Island, and references have been found for a number of others, which, unfortunately, do not seem to have survived. All these songs relate to events that occurred between 1812 and 1976.

Since many of these ballads involve a sudden death, the dominant theme is often of a religious nature. The poet and the community were haunted by the question as to whether people, taken suddenly from this world, would go to heaven. This concern is particularly obvious in the case of drownings. These accidents at sea were considered to be especially tragic because the victims died without being able to confess or receive the last rites. According to the teachings of the Catholic Church, a person who died in the state of mortal sin would go directly to hell, whereas someone who had committed venial sins could atone for his or her transgressions in purgatory before going to heaven. The authors of the ballads were afraid that the victims of these tragic deaths would not have had time to make peace with God before facing the almighty Judge. Given their concern with the fate of the dead, they often urged their audience to pray that the person's soul rest in peace.

Except for the somewhat sophisticated style that would suggest the work of a well-educated person, the song *Firmin Gallant* constitutes a good example of a ballad about a death at sea. It describes the drowning of a young fisherman from Rustico in 1862. Evidence indicates that he was born on February 14, 1844, the son of Joseph Gallant and Marie Blaquière.

The author of this ballad, whose identity is unknown, appeals to our feelings of pity and compassion. Not content simply to relate the events surrounding the tragedy, he (or she) gives the young Firmin Gallant a voice. In portraying the thoughts of the drowning man in his final moments, the author adds to the emotional impact of the song.

The following version was sung to me by Alma Arsenault, *née* LeClair (1901–1974), from St. Hubert in the parish of Egmont Bay. It was one of the ballads her mother used to sing.

Firmin Gallant

Original key: C major

C'est dans no - tre pe - tite î - le Nom-mée du nom de St -

Jean, De Rus - ti - co, quel-ques mil - les, J'en-tre - vois un cher en -

fant Dans u - ne pe-ti-te bar-que Du ri - vag' bien é - loi -

gné, Qui, par beau - coup de re - cher - ches,

Ses   fi - lets   s'en   va   cher - cher.

C'est dans notre petite île
Nommée du nom de Saint-Jean,
De Rustico, quelques milles,
J'entrevois un cher enfant
Dans une petite barque
Du rivag' bien éloigné,
Qui, par beaucoup de recherches,
Ses filets s'en va chercher.

Après beaucoup de recherches,
Ses filets il a trouvés,
Et tout hardiment il marche
D'un pas ferme et rassuré.
Et bientôt là, il s'embarque
Sur le bord de son vaisseau,
Et bientôt sa main si forte,
Le filet monta bien haut.

Survint une vague haute,
Le bateau a chaviré,
Au moins d'un mille de la côte
Ce cher enfant s'est noyé.
Étant au fond des abîmes
Ce cher enfant a crié :
« Dieu, qui mesurez l'abîme,
Ô daignez [me] délivrer. »

Ô l'entendez-vous, cher Père,
Ce cher enfant qui vous prie?
Ô nous le croyions donc guère
Qu'il perdrait sitôt la vie.
« Et vous, ô ma tendre Mère,
Qui habitez dans les cieux,
Par vos puissantes prières,
Arrachez-moi de ce lieu.

— Georges Arsenault

Ô Vierge, ô sainte ma Mère,
Ô daignez me secourir.
D'une aussi triste manière,
Ô mon Dieu, faut donc mourir!
Mon bon ange tutélaire,
Vous qui guidez tous mes pas,
Offrez à Dieu mes prières
Afin qu'il me perde pas.

Mon corps est la nourriture
De tous les monstres des eaux,
Comme il serait la pâture
Des vers au fond d'un tombeau.
Mais hélas! Qu'importe-t-il
Puisque l'âme est assurée,
Si des cieux, je trouve la porte
Ouverte pour y entrer.

En ce moment j'abandonne
Tous ceux que j'ai tant aimés.
Aux monstres marins je donne
Ce corps que j'ai tant flatté.
Que je laisse dans mes ondes
Mes os, mon sang et ma chair,
Et je vois bien que le monde
Est un séjour de malheur.

Je vous dis adieu, cher père,
Adieu parents et amis,
Adieu mes frères et mes soeurs
Que vous serez fort surpris
D'apprendre que dans ma force
Je me suis fait emporter
Comme une légère écorce
Que le vent souffle à son gré. »

Son corps pour quatre semaines
Est resté au fond des eaux.
Ses parents avec grande peine
Le cherchaient dans son tombeau.
Jour de juin, le vingt-troisième,

Mil huit cent soixante et deux,
Ce corps si pâle et si blême
Flottait sur ces eaux si bleues.

Il a les mains et la face
Cruellement massacrées,
Les poissons, cruelle race,
Les avaient toutes rongées.
C'est en grande cérémonie
Qu'on a fait l'enterrement,
Tandis que chacun le prie,
Le Seigneur Dieu tout-puissant.

Si vous désirez d'entendre
Le nom de ce cher enfant,
Je vais vous le faire comprendre,
Son nom est Firmin Gallant.
Dix-huit années est son âge,
Bien vigoureux et bien fort,
Plein de vie et de courage,
Se croyant loin de la mort.

Firmin Gallant

'Twas on our little island
Named St. John's Island,
From Rustico, several miles away,
I see a dear child
In a little fishing boat
Far from the shore,
Who is searching hard,
Trying to find his nets.

After searching hard,
He found his nets,
And bravely he walks
With a firm and confident step.
And soon, he climbs
On board his ship,
And soon with his strong hand,
Pulls the net high in the air.

A huge wave appeared,
The boat overturned,
At least a mile off shore
That dear child drowned.
From the bottom of the abyss
That dear child cried out,
"God, who measures the abyss,
Oh deign to deliver [me]."

Oh do you hear him, dear Father,
That dear child who begs you?
Oh we scarcely thought
He'd lose his life so soon.
"And you, oh my sweet Mother,
Who lives in heaven,
By your powerful prayers,
Wrench me from this place.

"Oh Blessed Virgin, Oh Holy Mother,
Oh deign to help me.
In such a sad manner,
Oh my Lord, must I die!
My good guardian angel,
You who guides my every step,
Give God my prayers
So He will not lose me.

"My body is food
For all the monsters in the sea,
As it would be the pasture
For worms in the depths of a tomb.
But alas! What does it matter
Since the soul is safe,
If in heaven, I find the door
Open for me to enter.

"And now I am leaving
All those I loved so much.
To the sea monsters I give
This body I have worked so hard

That I leave in my wake
My bones, my blood and my flesh,
And I now see that the world
Is a sojourn of misfortunes.

"I bid you farewell, dear father,
Farewell friends and relatives,
Farewell my brothers and my sisters.
You will be truly surprised
To learn that despite my strength
I was carried away
Like a piece of bark
Blown at will by the wind."

His body for four weeks
Did lie at the bottom of the sea.
His relatives with great pain
Searched for him in his tomb.
The twenty-third day of June,
Eighteen hundred sixty-two,
That body so pale and wan
Was floating on those waters so blue.

His hands and his face
So cruelly bruised,
The fish, cruel things,
Had chewed them up.
'Twas with great ceremony
That the burial was held,
While everyone prayed
God, the Father almighty.

If you wish to hear
The name of that dear child,
I will tell you,
His name is Firmin Gallant.
Eighteen years old he was,
Truly powerful and strong,
Full of life and courage,
Thinking he was far from death.[3]

Jérôme

The ballad on the death of the lumberjack Jérôme Maillet is one of the most widespread Acadian ballads from Prince Edward Island. Well-known by traditional singers on the Island, it has also been collected by folklorists in New Brunswick, Cape Breton, the Magdalen Islands, the Gaspé Peninsula, and Maine.

The youngest son of Anselme Maillet and Françoise Arsenault, Jérôme Maillet was born in St. Louis, in the parish of Palmer Road, on March 16, 1870. Like many young men of his time, he worked in lumbercamps on the mainland. In 1892, Jérôme, his brother Georges, and no doubt other Islanders, were working in an American lumbercamp located in Bethel, Maine. Jérôme was seriously hurt when the tree he was cutting fell on him. He was taken care of as best as possible for several months in the camp, but, given the medical facilities available, he died on April 5, 1892, at the age of 22. [4]

Laurent Doucet
(Georges Arsenault Collection)

Laurent Doucet (1847–1923), the author of this beautiful ballad commemorating Jérôme Maillet, was also from St. Louis. In 1870, Laurent married Bibianne Arsenault from Sainte-Marie-de-Kent, New Brunswick. They had 13 children, most of whom were born on the Island. The younger offspring, however, were born in Rogersville, New Brunswick, where Laurent and his wife moved on April 30, 1893, in the footsteps of a number of other Island Acadians in search of land and a better life. [5] When he was in Rogersville, Laurent Doucet composed another ballad, this time on the accidental death of Jean Richard in 1906. [6]

According to the newspaper, *The Examiner*, Laurent Doucet was an inventive man who attempted to create a "flying machine." He showed his invention in 1889 at the parish picnic in Palmer Road. At the time, a journalist wrote, "The burning question of the day, 'Can Man Fly?' was practically answered by Mr. Laurent Doucet... The invention of his flying machine is truly wonderful." [7] Whether Laurent Doucet actually succeeded in flying his airplane remains unknown, but because of his attempts he was nicknamed "*Oiseau*" (Bird).

One of the reasons the ballad on Jérôme Maillet spread so quickly is because it is a well-crafted song that makes a strong appeal to our emotions. The section in which Jérôme talks to his brother about his approaching death is particularly moving. One of Jérôme's great-nieces told me that she could not help crying every time she heard her mother sing this ballad while she was spinning.

The following version was sung to me in 1972 by Lucille Arsenault (1892–1996), a native of Abrams Village. She knew nothing about the lumberjack mentioned in the song except that his name was Jérôme and that he was from somewhere on the Island.

Écoutez, jeunes gens, ce triste récit
D'un brave gentilhomme, en quittant sa patrie,
Quittant si jeune encore ses parents et amis
Pour s'en aller au loin dans les États-Unis.

Parti de chez lui, c'est pour s'en aller
Dans les États-Unis, c'est pour y travailler.
Mais ce brave jeune homme pensait bien d'éviter
La mort si cruelle qui lui est destinée.

Un jour en travaillant, étant dans le bois,
Z-en abattant un arbre il a fait un faux pas.
Mais ce brave jeune homme croyait bien d'éviter
La chute de cet arbre qui vient de le frapper.

Eugène qui était là, le voyant inanimé,
Il a couru à lui, c'est pour le dégager.
Mais ainsi quel spectacle de voir tout ensanglanté,
Ce corps tout difforme aussi si meurtrié.

Il s'écrit : « Hélas! Mes très chers amis,
Venez, accourez vite car Jérôme s'est tué! »
Ses amis s'empressèrent et que virent-ils, hélas!
Ce corps tout aimable qui baignait dans son sang.

Ils l'ont pris tous les trois et l'ont transporté
Dans une petite campe qui n'est pas éloignée.
Il est sans connaissance et il y resta ainsi
Pendant deux jours entiers sans aucun signe de vie.

– Il nous faut, mes amis, oh! vite aller chercher
Le docteur le plus proche et l'amener ici.
Et le docteur alors, qu'ils ont tant désiré,
S'approche du malade, il est fort attristé.

– Je vous dis, mes amis, oh! je ne crois pas
Que ce brave jeune homme meure de cela.
Mais souvent l'homme de science s'est bien souvent trompé
Parce que deux mois plus tard il était décédé.

Auprès de son lit, son frère Georges est assis.
Il lui a dit : « Jérôme, regrettes-tu de mourir? »
– Tout ce que je regrette, cher frère, avant de mourir,
C'est de voir mon père, ma mère, qui m'avont tant chéri.

– Jérôme, console-toi car tu ne peux pas
Revoir ceux que tu veux voir, hélas! console-toi.
Car ceux que tu veux voir sont éloignés d'ici,
Mais espère de les voir un jour en paradis.

– Puisqu'il faut, cher frère, me soumettre à la mort,
Tu enverras mon corps, c'est dans notre pays.
Je voudrais en terre sainte y être enterré
Avec tous mes amis qui m'avont tant chéri.

Il a bien souffri pendant deux mois entiers
Sans pouvoir y revoir ceux qu'il désirait tant.
On appela un prêtre, on alla pour le qu'ri',
Il ne veut pas venir car c'est pas son pays.

Une lettre apprit à ses parents chéris
Que leur cher fils, Jérôme, venait de mourir.
Quel jour de larmes pour cette mère, hélas!
D'apprendre que son cher fils est passé au trépas.

Son désir enfin s'étant accompli,
À la suite de son frère, le ramenant chez lui.
Quel jour de larmes pour cette mère chérie
D'avoir son fils tout aimable mort et enseveli.

Se jetant à genoux : « Vierge, secourez-nous!
Prenez part à mes peines, car je m'adresse à vous.
Prenez part à mes peines, priez votre cher fils,
Que mon enfant en jouisse de son saint paradis. »

Jérôme

Listen, young people, to this sad tale
About a brave young man who left his homeland,
Leaving while still so young his parents and friends
To go to work far away in the United States.

Leaving home to go away
To the United States to work.
But this brave young man thought he could avoid
The cruel death that was his fate.

One day, while working in the woods,
While felling a tree, he stumbled.
But this brave young man thought he could avoid
The falling tree that hit him.

Seeing him lying motionless, Eugene
Ran to try and free him.
But what a sight to see covered with blood
That body all crippled and bruised.

He called out, "Alas, my dearest friends,
Come, run quickly because Jérôme's been killed!"
His friends hurried and what did they see, alas!
That beloved body soaked in blood.

The three men took him and carried him
To a little camp not far away.
He was unconscious and stayed that way
For two whole days without a sign of life.

—We must, my friends, run quickly to fetch
The nearest doctor and bring him here.
And the doctor, they needed so badly,
Bent over the sick man, he was saddened.

—I tell you, my friends, oh! I don't think
That brave young man will die from that.
But often the man of science makes mistakes
Because two months later he had passed away.

At his bedside, his brother George was sitting.
He said to him, "Jérôme, are you loath to die?"
—All that I regret, dear brother, is that before I die,
I will see neither my father nor my mother who cherished me so.

"Jérôme, take heart for you cannot
See those who you wish to see again, alas! take heart.
For those you wish to see are far from here,
But hope that you will see them one day in heaven.

—Since I must, dear brother, submit to death,
Send my body to our country.
I wish to be buried in holy ground
With all my friends who cherished me so.

He suffered more for two long months
Without being able to see those he loved so.
A priest was called, they went to fetch him,
He would not come for it was not his country.

A letter told his dear parents
That their beloved son, Jérôme, had died.
What a day of tears for that mother, alas!
To learn that her dear son had departed this life.

His wish was at last fulfilled,
His brother accompanied him home.
What a day of tears for that dear mother
To have her beloved son dead and enshrouded.

Kneeling, she cried, "Blessed Virgin, help us!
Share in my pain, I call to you.
Share in my pain, pray to your dear Son,
So that my child will enter His holy paradise."[8]

Paneau's Dog

One of the gems in the repertoire of Acadian songs composed on the Island
is called *Le chien à Paneau* ("Paneau's Dog"). It was composed around 1890
by a songmaker from Egmont Bay parish by the name of Thomas Arsenault
(1848–1924), better-known as Tom Magitte. He gained a reputation because
of his humourous satirical songs, several of which, including *Le chien à Paneau*,
served as a form of public admonishment.

The repertoire of native Acadian songs includes a fairly large number of
satirical compositions. Their main purpose was to put pressure on individuals
or groups who overstepped the social norms of the community. In other words,
these songs encouraged people to respect local customs and traditions.

Tom Magitte, born on December 21, 1848, was a well-known personality
in his area. He and his wife, Judith Arsenault, operated a small farm on

Line Road, located on the outskirts of the village of St. Chrysostome. The Arsenaults did not have any children of their own, but they brought up three orphan girls. Since the farm did not generate enough income to support the family, Tom Magitte worked during the fishing season at a lobster cannery belonging to Joseph Gallant, otherwise known as "Jos Paneau." The factory was not far from Tom Magitte's farm in the part of St. Chrysostome called the Barachois.

Thomas "Magitte" Arsenault seated with his wife Judith, with Jacqueline Arsenault standing. Photo taken in 1914 (Linda Fitzgerald Collection)

People who remember Tom Magitte all agree that he was a good singer. He was a member of the church choir. He was a cheerful man who liked to tease people, or, as Augustin J. Arsenault put it, "He had a sharp tongue, but it was more for fun than anything else. It wasn't to be mean." Since he was a Liberal, one of his greatest pleasures was to make up rhymes that ridiculed his political opponents.

Le chien à Paneau is a caustic song that is unquestionably one of his best compositions. It is set in Jos Paneau's factory and targets an employee by the name of Sylvain Caissie (1839–1901), nicknamed "Sylvain Pichi."[9] Tom Magitte accused him of stealing and killing Calbé, the boss' dog.

It would appear that the accused man did not have a good reputation in this devoutly Catholic community, because he had failed to respect his religious obligations. The 1890 parish census[10] indicates that he was the only parishioner not to have done his Easter duties.[11] The Catholic Church considered this an extremely serious violation and refused to allow anyone who died without having fulfilled this religious duty to be buried in the consecrated church cemetery. When criticizing Sylvain Pichi for his marginal lifestyle, Tom Magitte does not mince his words:

Pichi, si tu allais plus souvent
Recevoir les sacrements,
Tu vivrais bien plus en paix
Avec ta femme et tes enfants,
Tu aurais pas toujours l'idée
De tuer tous les Calbé.

Pichi, if you went more often
To receive the sacraments,
You would live much more peacefully
With your wife and children,
It wouldn't occur to you
To kill all the Calbés.[12]

Although Le chien à Paneau has been collected by several folklorists, the above verse has only been found in one version. Perhaps these lines were eliminated because it was felt that Tom Magitte's denunciation was somewhat exaggerated and that the other verses of his song constituted sufficient punishment.

This song spread to various parts of the Island, and even crossed the Northumberland Strait to become part of the repertoire of the traditional singers of St. Mary's Bay in southwest Nova Scotia. In fact, Marie-Marthe Dugas from Church Point is the only person to have recorded this song for an album.[13]

The novelist and playwright, Antonine Maillet, collected the following version in 1966 from 86-year-old Mélanie Arsenault who was living in Abrams Village. Mrs. Arsenault remembered Tom Magitte and Sylvain Pichi because she had spent several summers during her childhood in the Barachois area of St. Chrysostome, where her mother, who was a widow, worked in Jos Paneau's lobster cannery.

Le chien à Paneau

Original key: B♭ major

Venez en - ten - dre le ré - cit D'un app' - lé Sylvain Pi-

chi. Il a fait un tour sa - lop, Il a vo-

lé l'chien à Pa - neau. On dit qu'il l'a

fu - sil - lé, Dans sa cav', l'a d'a - mar - ré.

Venez entendre le récit
D'un appelé Sylvain Pichi.
Il a fait un tour salop.
Il a volé l'chien à Paneau.
On dit qu'il l'a fusillé,
Dans sa cav', l'a d'amarré.

Ce fut par un jeudi à midi,
Pichi arrive à la fact'rie.
Il dit qu'il a v'nu chercher
C'est un vaisseau pour goudronner,
Mais il avait dans son idée,
C'était d'emmener Calbé.

– Pichi, si t'avais su t'y prendre,
Tu l'aurais amené la nuit.
Là, personne aurait pu dire
Que c'est toi qui l'avais pris.
À présent, tout le monde dit :
« Encore un tour à Pichi. »

Si tu vas au confessionnal
Faire réparer ton scandale,
Là, l'bon curé te dira :
« Va-t-en payer ce beau chien-là,
Tu trouveras il faut payer chaud
Le beau chien à Jos Paneau. »

Si tu vas en paradis
Sans avoir payé l'plein prix,
Le bon saint Pierre te dira :
« Va-t-en là-bas dans l'trou d'en bas,
Tu trouveras qu'il coûte chaud
Le Calbé à Jos Paneau. »

Paneau's Dog

Come listen to the story
About a certain Sylvain Pichi.
He did a dirty trick.
He stole Paneau's dog.
They say he shot it,
Tied up in his cellar.

One Thursday at noon,
Pichi arrived at the factory.
He said he came to get
A tub to use for tarring,
But what he had in mind,
Was to take Calbé.

—Pichi, if you'd been smart,
You'd have taken it at night.
Then, nobody would be able to say
That it was you who took it.
Now, everyone says,
"Another one of Pichi's tricks."

If you go to confession
To have your scandal pardoned,
Then, the good priest will tell you,
—Go pay for that handsome dog,
You'll find you'll pay dearly
For Jos Paneau's handsome dog.

If you go to heaven
Without paying the full price,
Good Saint Peter will tell you,
—Go down there into the hole,
You'll find you'll pay dearly
For Jos Paneau's Calbé. [14]

Marie Caissie around 1920
(Judy Bellefontaine Collection)

Marie Caissie

The aim of a satirical song is not always obvious if one is not aware of the context. Is a song designed to mock or simply to tease? On reading the words of Marie Caissie, one might think that the author wanted to ridicule this spinster from Palmer Road, who apparently was as thin as a rake. However, according to people who knew Marie Caissie (1873–1922), that was not the purpose of the song. She is remembered as a kind person, always in a pleasant mood and who had a good sense of humour. Her former neighbour, Évangéline Allain, said that Marie Caissie would not have been offended by the song; in fact, she would have found it amusing.

What did Marie Caissie do to merit a song? It was not so much what she did, but what happened to her. Around 1920, she went with other members of her family to Henry Doucette's place to celebrate Shrove Tuesday. The meal included *chiard*, a traditional Acadian dish made with grated potatoes. One of my informants told me that Marie Caissie suffered from diarrhea or intestinal problems caused by a tapeworm. In any case, she left the party before the other members of the family in order to put wood in the stove. On her way home, she was suddenly struck by the urge to relieve herself. She went into the privacy of a little wooded area beside the road but, unfortunately, the poor woman sank into the snow and remained stuck until John Poirier, the church caretaker, came along and rescued her. Rita Perry describes how her father discovered Marie Caissie:

> He had his lantern. He had set out in a storm to light the furnace
> [in the church]. When he was not far from the Caissies' place
> he heard a wailing sound between gusts of wind. What's that? A
> sound sort of like, Aaaaaaaah... He went closer to the fence, but
> he sank into the snow, it was so deep. He found Marie uncon-
> scious, half-dead. [...] He had to pull her out, he dragged her out
> of there... So, he saved her life. If she'd been there a little bit longer,
> she'd have been dead. She'd already started to freeze.[15]

Even though she was only five years old at the time, Alice Doucette, Marie Caissie's niece, remembers the event very clearly. She said that when the other members of the family got back to the house, they had not given Marie a thought since they assumed she had gone to bed. "They heard someone knocking at the door. My grandfather opened the door and saw John Poirier with my aunt Marie on his shoulder. She was unconscious. [...] They laid her down on the sofa and warmed her up with a wool blanket."

It was not long before the story of Marie Caissie's misadventure had spread throughout the parish. People were still talking about it the following summer when Minnie Pitre (Mrs. Benjamin Maillet, 1883–1975) returned from the United States to visit her family and friends in Palmer Road. In fact, it was she who immortalized the Marie Caissie story in verse. Little did she know that one day her amusing song would appear on a record and be sung at the Olympia, the famous music hall in Paris! The song has travelled far and wide, thanks to Édith Butler,[16] who discovered a recording of it sung by Léo Gallant (1912–1986) in Arichat, Cape Breton. He was born in Tignish, Prince Edward Island. Apparently the original song had several verses that are missing from Léo Gallant's version.

Marie Caissie

Original key: E♭ minor

1er couplet

Ah ! c'est Ma - rie   Cais - sie,   bi - bi

botteun', Elle a 'té   veil - ler,   bi - bi

botteun'   Sus Hen - e - ry,   bi - bi

2e couplet

botteun' a - la - wé !   Au com -

menc' - ment d'la   soi - rée,   bi - bi

botteun' Y'a com-men- cé   à   nei - ger,   bi - bi,

botteun' a - la - wé !   Ma - rie a point vou - lu   res -

Acadian Legends, Folktales, and Songs from Prince Edward Island — 126

ter,   bi - bi   botteun' Peur de s'é - car -

ter,   bi - bi   botteun' a - la- wé !

Ah! c'est Marie Caissie, *bibi botteune,*
Elle a 'té veiller, *bibi botteune,*
Sus Henery, *bibi botteune alawé,*

Au commenc'ment d'la soireé, *bibi botteune,*
Y a commencé à neiger, *bibi botteune alawé.*
Marie a point voulu rester, *bibi botteune,*
Peur de s'écarter, *bibi botteune alawé.*

Elle a pris en travers, *bibi botteune,*
Elle avait la foire, *bibi botteune alawé.*
Elle a pris d'un péteau, *bibi botteune,*
Elle a fait son eau, *bibi botteune alawé.*

Elle a 'té dans la bouillée, *bibi botteune,*
Elle s'a embourbée, *bibi botteune alawé.*
Elle a yuché : « Fayelle, *bibi botteune,*
Apportez des pelles, » *bibi botteune alawé.*

Ils ont couri à yelle, *bibi botteune,*
Avec des pelles, *bibi botteune alawé.*
Ils l'ont 'ttrapée par les deux jambes, *bibi botteune.*
Y avait point grand viande, *bibi botteune alawé.*

Mais y avait un glaçon, *bibi botteune,*
Au bout des talons, *bibi botteune alawé.*
Ah! ils l'ont mis' au lit, *bibi botteune,*
Trois jours et trois nuits, *bibi botteune alawé.*

Marie Caissie

Ah! it's Marie Caissie, *beebee button*,
She went to party, *beebee button*,
At Henery's place, *beebee button allaway*,

In the early evening, *beebee button*,
It started to snow, *beebee button allaway*.
Marie didn't want to stay, *beebee button*,
Afraid of getting lost, *beebee button allaway*.

She took a short cut, *beebee button*,
She had the runs, *beebee button allaway*.
She held on to a post, *beebee button*,
She had a leak, *beebee button allaway*.

She went into a thicket, *beebee button*,
She got stuck, *beebee button allaway*.
She yelled, "Fayelle,[17] *beebee button*,
Bring the shovels," *beebee button allaway*.

They ran to her, *beebee button*,
With their shovels, *beebee button allaway*.
They took her by both legs, *beebee button*.
She didn't have much flesh, *beebee button allaway*.

But there were icicles, *beebee button*,
On her heels, *beebee button allaway*.
Ah! they put her to bed, *beebee button*,
For three days and three nights, *beebee button allaway*.[18]

The Big Sow

The singer Florence Bernard,[19] from Abrams Village, born in 1916, has composed numerous songs over the years, but *La grand' truie* ("The Big Sow") is by far her best. She composed it around 1930 and has sung it hundreds of times since then. In fact, no kitchen party she attends would be complete without her performing it while accompanying herself on the harmonium or the piano. In 1981, she was even recorded during a live concert of Acadian music for the album called *Comment ça flippe*[20] (*How's It Going*).

The song relates a true story that happened to Florence's family. Her father, Emmanuel Aucoin, died in an accident, leaving his wife Mélanie (1881–1972) alone with three young children. After remaining a widow for several years, she married Ferdinand Arsenault, a widower and farmer from Abrams Village. He and his first wife had not had any children, but they had raised two orphans.

Mélanie Arsenault and her grandchildren, Della and André Bernard, around 1948 (Florence Bernard Collection)

Generous and hard-working, Mélanie was not an imposing woman physically, but she had a strong personality and indomitable courage. Ferdinand, a well-known storyteller in the area, was not one to exert himself unduly, often leaving Mélanie to do all the barn chores by herself. Florence and her sister felt that their stepfather did not take his full share of the responsibilities on the farm and, above all, did not appreciate the true value of their mother's hard work. This was confirmed when Mélanie took care of the piglets after the big sow died. Florence described in the following manner the circumstances that inspired her to compose her song *La grand'truie* ("The Big Sow").

> When she went to the barn in the morning, the big sow was dead. Ferdinand wanted to let the little pigs die, but she said to him, "No, we can't do that." She took them into the house and fed them milk and molasses with a spoon. She got up every hour during the night and got her little pigs to drink. She managed to save enough of them to make a few bucks.
>
> After the weather warmed up, they put them out in the barn. When they grew to be big pigs, they sold them. Ferdinand sold them. With the money, he and José Prosse [his adopted son] each bought a big fur coat. So my mother got zero. That's what she got paid. She did all the work, but she didn't get anything, not even a thank you![21]

This glaring injustice inspired Florence and her sister Léna to compose a song criticizing their stepfather's unacceptable behaviour. Fifty years after the event, Florence said, "I think I was mad at the time. But, after a while, we just joked about it." In fact, she could even sing the song in front of Ferdinand, which obviously proved that he was not all that bad.

La grand' truie

Original key: A major

C'est la grand'truie à sus Fer - di- nand, Qu'a eu qua - torz'
p'tits co-chans. Mé - la - nie é - tait dé - montée En
vo - yant un' pa - reill' cou vée. Ell' dit : C'est - y
pas dom- mage Y'en a deux qu'ont fait naufrag'.

C'est la grand' truie à sus Ferdinand,
Qu'a eu quatorz' p'tits cochans.
Mélanie était démontée
En voyant une pareille couvée.
Ell' dit : « C'est-y pas dommage
Y en a deux qu'ont fait naufrage. »

Le jeudi après-midi
À la grange s'en va Mélanie.
Elle entra et elle trouva
La grand' truie qui était corvée.
Elle dit : « C'est-y pas décourageant »,
En voyant une pareille accident.

Elle a pris ces douze p'tits cochans-là,
À la cuillère elle les éleva.
Mais par une belle matinée
Il y en a trois qui ont corvé.
Elle dit : « Y m'en reste encore neuf,
Je pense bien que c'est assez. »

Avec ces neuf p'tits cochans,
Elle pensait d'y faire d'l'argent.
Mais vous connaissez Ferdinand,
C'est lui qu'a eu le paiement.
Il dit : « T'auras honte assez,
De l'argent tu vas t'en passer. »

Mélanie, vous la connaissez,
Vous savez qu'elle est pas gênée.
Elle dit : « Quand j'aurons une autre truie
Qui corv'ra comme celle-ci,
T'élèvera les p'tits cochans
Si tu veux avoir l'argent! »

The Big Sow

It was the big sow at Ferdinand's,
Who had fourteen little pigs.
Mélanie was delighted, seeing a litter like that.
She said, "Isn't it too bad
That two of them perished."

On Thursday afternoon
Off to the barn goes Mélanie.
She went in and saw
That the old sow had died.
She said, "Isn't it discouraging,
Seeing an accident like that."

131— Georges Arsenault

She took the twelve little pigs,
She raised them by the spoonful.
But one fine morning
Three of them died.
She said, "I've still got nine left,
I think that's good enough."

With those nine little pigs,
She thought she'd make some money.
But you know Ferdinand,
'Twas he who got the pay.
He said, "I'll show you who's boss!
You'll go without the money."

Mélanie, you know her,
She isn't shy, you understand.
She said, "When we have another sow
Who dies like that one,
You'll raise the little pigs
If you want to pocket the money!"[22]

On Halloween

Aside from ballads and satirical songs, the Acadian repertoire contains numerous local compositions more closely related to daily life. The songs refer not only to amusing incidents, but to memorable events that took place in the community, in a family, or amongst a group of friends.

The song called *La veille de la Toussaint* ("On Halloween") originates from Palmer Road parish. Neither the author nor the exact circumstances surrounding the song are known. It was probably composed at the beginning of the 20th century by a young man who tells how he and his friends stole geese from several parishioners at various times during the year. Were geese really stolen, or is the song just a pretext for making up rhymes about popular celebrations and parishioners' names? Were there other verses? This intriguing little enumerative song was sung to me by Alyre Chaisson from Summerside. He had learned it from his mother, Maggie Chaisson, when he was living in St. Edward.

La veille de la Toussaint

Original key: D major

La veill' de la Tous - saint   Les pi -

rounes à Syl - vain   Coin,   Ils   ont toutes 'té   vo -

lé   -   es.   Et   pis man - gées !

La veille de la Toussaint
Les pirounes à Sylvain Coin[23],
Ils ont toutes 'té volées.
Et pis mangées!

La veille de Noël
Les pirounes au vieux Madrelle
Ils ont toutes 'té volées
Et pis mangées.

La veille du premier d'l'An
Les pirounes à Pierre Gallant
Ils avont 'té volées
Et pis mangées.

La veille de Pâques
Quand les pirounes à George Knox
Ils ont toutes 'té volées
Et pis mangées.

On Halloween

On All Saints' Eve
Sylvain Coin's geese,
Were all stolen.
And then eaten!

On Christmas Eve
Old Madrelle's geese
Were all stolen
And then eaten.

On New Year's Eve
Pierre Gallant's geese
Were all stolen
And then eaten.

On Easter Eve
George Knox's geese
Were all stolen
And then eaten.[24]

And You Hear Me Well

Composed in the early 1930s, *Et vous m'entendez bien* ("And You Hear Me Well"), like the preceeding song, originates from the parish of Palmer Road. It relates the misadventure of a group of friends whose car went off the road and landed in the ditch. The accident took place one autumn night, when the dirt roads had turned to mud.

The song describes Caliste and Adèle Maillet from Leoville, and their friends, Magitte (Jack) and Marie-Anne Arsenault, who had come from Bloomfield parish for a visit. One evening, the two couples decided to go to St. Edward to see Françoise and Léon Poirier. As the song indicates, everyone had a good time during the evening, but, on returning home, the Arsenaults and the Maillets had an unpleasant surprise.

Their accident was immortalized in song by a songmaker and fisherman from Deblois by the name of Isaïe (à Pitro) Bernard (1875–1941).[25] Although he did not actually witness the accident, it did not take long before he heard about it. Since Isaïe was always on the lookout for unusual events, he seized on the occasion to compose a new humourous song. His composition was so successful that many people learned it. As a result, it spread to several villages in the western part of the Island. I collected the following version in St. Louis from Nellie Luttrell, *née* Perry (1909–1993).

Et vous m'entendez bien

Original key B♭ major

Par un' bell' soi - rée a - près sou - per, Ca - liste et A - dèle ont 'té veil - ler. Dans le *car* à Mad - gitte, Et vous bien, Con - duit par Ma - rie - Anne, Et vous m'en - ten - dez bien.

Par une belle soirée après souper, }
Caliste et Adèle ont 'té veiller. } *bis*
Dans le car à Magitte,
Et vous bien,
Conduit par Marie-Anne,
Et vous m'entendez bien.

C'est sus Léon qu'ils ont été }
En pensant d'avoir une bonne soirée. } *bis*
Il y avait assez d'quoi à manger,
Et vous bien,

Et un p'tit peu d'alké
Et vous m'entendez bien.

C'était en v'nant sur les minuits,   }
Magitte a dit : « Faut prendre le chemin. } *bis*
Nous prendrons notre temps,
Et vous bien,
Car c'est terriblement coulant,
Et vous m'entendez bien. »

C'est quand qu'ils avont arrivé sus Jean Xavier, }
C'est dans l'canal qu'ils s'avont j'tés.   } *bis*
Ils avont r'venu sus leur côté,
Et vous bien,
Les femmes ont débarqué,
Et vous m'entendez bien.

Adèle embrassa Marie-Anne   }
En se recommandant à sainte Anne } *bis*
J'avons pas attrapé de mal,
Et vous bien,
Ramassions nos médalles,
Et vous m'entendez bien.

C'est sus Mokler qu'ils ont été }
C'est pour se faire arracher   } *bis*
Dans toute son travail,
Et vous bien,
Caliste a perdu sa blague,
Et vous m'entendez bien.

Quand qu'ils avont arrivé sus Céleste }
Les voilà encore dans la tristesse   } *bis*
Ils avont venu sur leur côté.
Et vous bien,
Les femmes ont bostchulé,
Et vous m'entendez bien.

Adèle a dit : « J'débarquerai }
Et à mon pied je reprendrai. } *bis*
Je me rendrai au chemin à Pitre,

Et vous bien,
Que le diable emporte Magitte,
Et vous m'entendez bien. »

Caliste, sa blague a 'té remis' }
Par un de ses plus grands amis. } *bis*
C'était pas un avocat,
Et vous bien,
Mais par son frère François,
Et vous m'entendez bien.

And You Hear Me Well

One nice evening after supper, }
Caliste and Adèle went visiting. } x 2
In Magitte's car,
And you well,
With Marie-Anne at the wheel,
And you hear me well.

They went to Léon's place   }
Thinking they'd have a nice evening. } x 2
There was lots to eat,
And you well,
And a bit of liquor
And you hear me well.

It was around midnight when   }
Magitte said, "We must be on our way. } x 2
We'll take our time,
And you well,
Because it's awful slippery,
And you hear me well."

It was when they got to Jean Xavier's }
That they landed in the ditch.   } x 2
The car landed on its side,
And you well,
The women got out,
And you hear me well.

Adèle hugged Marie-Anne   }
All the while praying to Saint Anne } x 2
We didn't get hurt,
And you well,
Let's pick up our medals,
And you hear me well.

They went to Mokler's place }
For help to get pulled out   } x 2
In all his effort,
And you well,
Caliste lost his pouch,
And you hear me well.

When they got to Céleste's place }
Once again they were in distress } x 2
The car landed on its side.
And you well,
The women were tossed about,
And you hear me well.

Adèle said, "I'll get out }
And I'll go on by foot. } x 2
I'll go as far as Peter Road,
And you well,
The hell with Magitte,
And you hear me well."

Caliste's pouch was given back to him }
By one of his greatest friends.   } x 2
It wasn't a lawyer,
And you well,
But his brother François,
And you hear me well.[26]

Élizée and Tosie

The birth of twins never goes unnoticed in any small community, and when the parents have been married for 25 years and already have 12 children, one might think the event would be really newsworthy. However, in 1949 large families were not rare on Prince Edward Island, so the arrival of twin boys in the household of Élizée and Théodosie (Tosie) Arsenault in Maximeville did not warrant any press coverage. Tosie's mother, a singer and songmaker from Mont Carmel named Madeleine (à Lamand) Richard, felt that the event was at least worth a song.

Madeleine Richard
(Collection Georges Arsenault)

The twins in question, Gérard and Edgar Arsenault, were born on November 3, 1949. The parents might have preferred two more girls since they already had ten boys. The oldest daughter, Marguerite, who was forced to leave school at a young age to help her mother with the housework, remembers the birth of her twin brothers very clearly. She admits that everybody was very surprised, although neither her mother nor the rest of the family were particularly disturbed by the event. Her 41-year-old mother was used to babies and the never-ending work associated with a large family.

During the course of her long life, the twins' grandmother, Madeleine Richard, *née* Arsenault (1880–1974),[27] composed a variety of songs, including one ballad on the drowning of the lobster fisherman, Arsène Arsenault, in 1935, and another one on Father Emmanuel Richard's ordination in 1949. At the age of 90, knowing that her years were numbered, she decided to compose a farewell song, asking her friends and relatives not to forget her after her death.[28] At 93, she still enjoyed singing and had an excellent memory, as the following lyrics indicate.

Élizée et Tosie

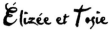

Original key: B♭ major

Ve- nez en - ten - dre le ré - cit, C'est d'É -
li - zée et To - sie. Quoi c'qu'a 'té trou- vé l'plus
beau, Ils a - vont un' pair' de ju- meaux. Moi, j'vous
dis, en vé - ri - té, Ça, c'é - tait pas leurs pre- miers.

Venez entendre le récit,
C'est d'Élizée et Tosie.
Quoi c'qu'a 'té trouvé l'plus beau,
Ils avont une paire de jumeaux.
Moi, j'vous dis, en vérité,
Ça, c'était pas leurs premiers.

Si j'pouvais additionner,
Je pourrais vous les nommer.
Mais en travaillant dans ma tête,
Je crois qu'ils en avont seize.
Moi, j'vous dis, en vérité,
Ça, c'est une grande famille assez!

— Élizée, si tu prends pas garde à toi,
La limite que tu casseras;
Et si ça va au gouvernement,
Ça fera un grand parlement,
Et si tu es promoté,
Ça prendra les délégués.

Ils disent que dans l'paradis
Les grandes familles sont plus élevées.
Mais Élizée, si tu y vas,
Oui, prends ben garde à toi.
Si tu tombes du haut en bas,
Prends ben garde que Tosie ne soit pas là.

Quand la journée va arriver
Que l'Père des cieux va t'appeler,
Le bon saint Pierre te dira :
« Eh! viens ici, mon p'tit Magat,
Tu as trop bien travaillé,
J'pouvons pas t'mettre à côté! »

Élizée and Tosie

Come listen to the story,
About Élizée and Tosie.
What was the most surprising,
They had a pair of twins.
I tell you in truth
That they weren't their first.

If I could add,
I could name them for you.
But working it out in my head,
I think they had sixteen.[29]
I tell you in truth,
That's a big enough family!

— Élizée, if you're not careful,
You'll break the record;
And if the government finds out,

That'll create a commotion,
And if you are to be rewarded,
You'll need the Members' help.

They say that in heaven
Large families are in the highest position.
But Élizée, if you go there,
You be careful.
If you fall from on high,
Be careful that Tosie isn't down below.

When the day comes
That our Father in heaven calls for you,
Good Saint Peter will say to you,
"Eh! come here my little Magat,
You've worked so hard,
We can't just put you aside!"[30]

The New Factory

Unlike the birth of Élizée and Tosie Arsenault's twins, the construction of a new fish plant in Abrams Village in 1971 attracted the attention of the media. The opening of this cannery represented an important event in the economic development of a region dominated by the fishing industry. Replacing the old lobster factory built in 1938, the new building enabled the fishermen's co-operative to increase its production and incorporate a large cold-storage warehouse.[31]

Florence Bernard in 1961 (Florence Bernard Collection)

The Acadian Fishermen's Cooperative Association Ltd. included fishermen not only from the parishes of Egmont Bay and Mont Carmel but also from several other communities in Prince County, so this project represented a major undertaking. It was only after considerable encouragement from government authorities and representatives of the Maritime Fishermen's Union that the members of the Co-op finally gave their go-ahead for the project on February 20, 1970.

Thanks to a federal government financial aid program, construction of the plant began in the fall of 1970. The work took place on schedule so that the $700,000 factory would be finished in August 1971, in time for the opening of the lobster season.[32]

One night in 1975 when she was having trouble falling asleep, Florence Bernard composed the following song called *La nouvelle facterie* ("The New Factory"). She wanted, above all, to pay tribute to the members of the Co-op and their energetic manager, Ulric Poirier, for their initiative, which had resulted in the creation of many new jobs in the area. On a more personal level, the Fishermen's Cooperative was the main source of income for several of Florence's children.

La nouvelle facterie

Original key: F# major

C'est dans l'an-née soix-ante et on - ze, C'est dans l'an-
née soix-ante et on - ze, Dans le p'tit Vil-lag' - des - A-
bram, J'vous dis qu'les pê - cheurs march'nt de l'a - vant.

C'est dans l'année soixante et onze, *(bis)*
Dans le p'tit Village-des-Abram,
J'vous dis qu'les pêcheurs marchent de l'avant.

C'est les pêcheurs d'la coopérative, *(bis)*
Avec Ulric à leurs côtés,
Ils ont dit : « Nous faut une autre facterie. »

Ils ont commencé à planner, *(bis)*
À planner et à travailler,
Et aussi à assister aux assemblées.

Voilà, la nouvelle qui s'épâre (*bis*)
Que la demande a été acceptée;
Mais c'est Ulric qu'ils doivent remercier.

C'est au printemps qu'l'ouvrage commence, (*bis*)
Une centaine d'hommes sont employés;
J'vous dis qu'l'ouvrage, ça va marcher.

Ils ont été obligé(e)s (*bis*)
De renforcer l'électricité
Pour pouvoir suffire à la grosse facterie.

Les pêcheurs qui se sont mis ensemble (*bis*)
Viennent de Mont-Carmel et d'Egmont-Baie,
Il y en a d'autres, bien plus éloignés.

Maintenant ma chanson vient d'finir(e), (*bis*)
Espérant que l'bon Dieu les bénira,
Et du poisson, il y en aura.

The New Factory

It was in the year nineteen seventy-one, x 2
In little Abrams Village,
I tell you the fishermen were moving ahead.

It was the fishermen from the co-operative, x 2
With Ulric at their side,
They said, "We need another factory."

They started planning, x 2
Planning and working,
And going to meetings.

And then news spread x 2
That the project had been accepted;
But it's Ulric they have to thank,

It was in spring that work began, x 2
A hundred men were hired;
I tell you the work was going ahead.

They were forced x 2
To upgrade the electricity
To be able to supply the big factory.

The fishermen who got together x 2
Came from Mont Carmel and Egmont Bay,
There were others from much farther away.

And now my song is ended, x 2
Here's hoping the good Lord will bless them,
And that there'll be lots of fish.[33]

The Calumets

Sometimes local songs are very long, like ballads, but they can also be very short. Such is the case of the following song, which pays tribute to the Calumet family. Calumet was the nickname of Cyprien Gallant, who married Marie Bernard in Egmont Bay on February 12, 1821.[34] The couple established their home in the area, which later became the village of St. Phillip and they had fourteen children, three of whom died at an early age.

In the past, many Acadians had nicknames. This was particularly useful in communities in which there were only two or three surnames. In the parishes of Egmont Bay and Mont Carmel, for example, the Gallants and the Arsenaults accounted for—and still do—over 60 per cent of the population.

Cyprien Gallant, known as "Calumet," was not the only member of his family to have a nickname. His father, Firmin Gallant, was better known as "Paneau," his brother Lamand had the nickname "Cannon," and his son, also named Lamand, was called "Blague." (A *blague* is a little pouch for the tobacco used in the type of pipe called a *calumet*. When referring to a pipe made of wood, Acadians used the word *calumet*, as opposed to the word *pipe*, which referred to a white clay pipe.[35]) Today these nicknames are still used to identify the many descendants of the various branches of this huge Gallant family.

Les Calumet is a short enumerative song that lists, in the order of their birth, the parents and all the surviving children in the Calumet Gallant family. Antoine Gallant from St. Phillip — the son of Pierre, Marie and Calumet's youngest child — might be the author of this song about his "remarkable family." It was sung to me by a descendant of Pélien, Imelda Arsenault, *née* Gallant (1915–1989), who was living in Abrams Village.

Les Calumet

Original key: B♭ major

Sa - lut, gloire à Ma - rie, La fa - mill' des Ca - lu-

met. Au jourd' hui, c'est Ma - rie qu'est

la plus vieille, Et en suit' c'est Ca - lu - met.

C'est un' fa - mill' re - mar qua - ble : So - phiq', Mar - cel -

lin', Mad'-lein', La - mand, Sa - ra, Ma - rie, Mar - gue- rit', Phi - lo -

mèn', Am brois', Pé - lien et Pier - re.

Salut, gloire à Marie,
La famille des Calumet.
Aujourd'hui c'est Marie qu'est la plus vieille,
Et ensuite c'est Calumet.
C'est une famille remarquable :
Sophique, Marcelline, Madeleine, Lamand,
Sara, Marie, Marguerite, Philomène,
Ambroise, Pélien et Pierre.

The Calumets

Hail, glory to Marie,
The Calumet family.
Today it's Marie who's the oldest,
Next comes Calumet.
It's a remarkable family:
Sophique, Marcelline, Madeleine, Lamand,
Sara, Marie, Marguerite, Philomène,
Ambroise, Pélien and Pierre.[36]

The 10 songs presented in this chapter originate from several Acadian villages in Prince Edward Island and describe events that took place between 1862 and 1971, thus covering a period of over a century. Little did the men and women who composed these songs know that they were documenting life in their community for future generations.

These songs mirror many aspects of traditional Acadian society. As unique documents and creative works by ordinary people, often with very little education, these samples of oral literature are extremely precious. In addition to describing local events, they offer a wealth of information on the mentality and social life of Island Acadians over a long period of time.

As we read or hear these songs, we have the impression of both seeing and savouring life in the Acadian community on the Island. The ballads enable us to share in the pain and compassion of people who have suffered tragedies. Other songs show us a close-knit and carefully controlled society, in which humour served as a useful tool for criticizing individuals whose behaviour deviated not only from the accepted social norm, but also from local customs and traditions. And the anecdotal songs, also with a good dose of humour, give us an insight into people's daily lives, a glimpse of their *joie de vivre* and their affection for both family and community.

Notes

[1] For a detailed study of both these ballads, see Georges Arsenault, *Complaintes acadiennes de l'île-du-Prince-Édouard*, Montréal: Leméac, 1980, pp. 93–168.

[2] Georges Arsenault, *Par un dimanche au soir : Léah Maddix, chanteuse et conteuse acadienne*, Moncton: Éditions d'Acadie, 1993, p. 48.

[3] Georges Arsenault Collection, Centre d'études acadiennes, Université de Moncton, Recording 23, 29 December 1971. Laforte: VI.C.3 *Gallant (Firmin)*. This ballad is sung to the tune of the folksong *Le cou de ma bouteille* (II.Q.19), and to the tune of the hymn *Au sang qu'un dieu va répandre*.

[4] Death certificate of Jerry Myers, born in Bethel, Maine, 5 April 1892. Department of Human Services, Augusta, Maine. Today, many of the Maillets on PEI go by Myers, the anglicized version of their name.

[5] *L'Impartial*, 3 May 1893, p. 3.

[6] Georges Arsenault Collection, CEA, Recording 1267, 28 March 1977

[7] "Tignish Notes," *The Examiner*, 12 August 1889, p. 2.

[8] Georges Arsenault Collection, CEA, Recording 19, 19 May 1971. Lucille Arsenault learned this ballad in her youth, but to refresh her memory she sang it using a manuscript provided by Alma Arsenault from St. Gilbert. Laforte: II.L.47, *Le bûcheron écrasé par un arbre*. Tune: II.E.16, *Les amants séparés par le père et la mère*. A version of this ballad, sung by Michel Faubert, is included on the recording *Voyage musical Québec*, Auvidis/Silex 1994, YA 225705.

[9] The father of Sylvain, Mathias Caissie, was a native of Richibouctou, New Brunswick, and was nicknamed "Pichi." He settled in Egmont Bay around 1830.

[10] Archives of the Diocese of Charlottetown.

[11] In other words, to have received communion given to the faithful by the Church between Ash Wednesday and Quasimodo Sunday.

[12] Soeur Antoinette DesRoches Collection, Centre d'études acadiennes, Université de Moncton, Manuscript 46, not dated.

[13] *Le temps de vivre*, Vol. 1, SELECT, SSP-24.246. In a letter dated 7 April 1980, Mrs. Dugas informed me that she had learned the song, which she called *Le chien à Pichi*, from her grandparents. She did not know that it came from PEI.

[14] Antonine Maillet Collection, Archives de folklore, Université Laval, Recording 152, 23 June 1966. Tune: IV.M2.46, *Les cartes*.

[15] Georges Arsenault Collection, CEA, Recording 1590, 2 April 1991.

[16] See Edith Butler's recordings: *Asteur qu'on est là...*, SPPS. PS-19905, 1979, and *Édith Butler à Paquetville*, SPPS, PS-19911, 1980.

[17] Marie's brother, Raphaël Caissie.

[18] Georges Arsenault Collection, CEA, Recording 1015, 7 August 1975.

[19] *Née* Aucoin, Florence Bernard married Joseph Bernard in 1935. They had six children.

[20] *Comment ça flippe*, Les productions de l'Île, Île 1002, 1981. This song is called *Mélanie* on the recording.

[21] Georges Arsenault Collection, CEA, Recording 1561, 3 May 1991.

[22] *Ibid.*, Tune: IV.Ma.46, *Les cartes*.

[23] Sylvain Aucoin from St. Louis

[24] Georges Arsenault Collection, CEA, Recording 1765, 27 May 1993.

[25] Isaïe Bernard married Élisabeth Poirier in 1900 and they had one child. His second wife was Fidélice Arsenault and they had four children.

[26] Georges Arsenault Collection, CEA, Recording 347, 5 June 1973. Tune: IV.N.11, *Vous m'entendez bien*.

[27] *Née* Madeleine Arsenault, she married Amand (Lamand) Richard in 1902. They had four children.

[28] Georges Arsenault, *Complaintes acadiennes de l'Île-du-Prince-Édouard, op. cit.,* pp. 55–58.

[29] Mrs. Richard included two children who died at a very young age.

[30] Georges Arsenault Collection, CEA, Recording 256, 24 May 1973. Tune: IV. Ma. 46, *Les cartes*.

[31] See Cécile Gallant, *Le mouvement coopératif chez les Acadiens de la région Évangéline* (1862–1982), Wellington: Conseil coopératif de l'Île-du-Prince-Édouard, 1982, p. 196.

[32] Anonymous article, "Abram's Village Plant to Open," *The Journal-Pioneer,* 10 August 1971.

[33] Georges Arsenault Collection, CEA, Recording 290, 30 May 1975. Tune: II.E.6, *Amant, je t'aime encore*.

[34] Patrice Gallant, *Michel Haché-Gallant et ses descendants,* Vol. 2, Sayabec, 1970, p. 46.

[35] Pascal Poirier, *Le glossaire acadien,* Critical edition by Pierre M. Gérin, Moncton: Éditions d'Acadie, 1994, p. 76.

[36] Georges Arsenault Collection, CEA, Recording 999, 6 August 1975.

Voices from the lamplight...

Bibliography

Bibliography

Georges Arsenault Collection

A. Recordings

Most of the recordings mentioned in this book are available for consultation at the Centre d'études acadiennes at the Université de Moncton.

Informants

Allain, Denise: 161, 182
Arsenault, Agnès et Willie: 688
Arsenault, Aldine: 1658
Arsenault, Alma: 23
Arsenault, Charles M.: 1176
Arsenault, Clothilde: 392, 393
Arsenault, Delphine: 1064, 1065
Arsenault, Henri: 1540
Arsenault, Imelda: 999
Arsenault, Amable: 1110
Arsenault, Lucille: 19
Arsenault, Stanley: 1238
Bernard, Florence: 290, 1201, 1561
Blacquière, Émilie: 666
Boisvert, Ozélie: 1497
Buote, Jean-François: 579
Chaisson, Alyre: 1375, 1388, 1622, 1623, 1626, 1628, 1757-1760, 1765
Chaisson, Alyre et Sarah: 1379, 1753
Chaisson, Anita: 1618
Chaisson, Émile: 1779 and cassette 48
Chaisson, James: 1750, 1752
Chaisson, Maggie: 114, 166, 180, 385, and cassette 48
Chaisson, Sarah: 1667
Chaisson-Pendergast, Eileen: 1612
DesRoches, Benoît: 1208
Doucette, Anna: recording not numbered
Doucette, Josie: 1454
Gallant, Léah: 447

Gallant, Léo: 1015
Gallant, Marie-Anne: 979, 986, 1023, 1458, 1643, 1644, 1648, and cassette 48
Gaudet, Emmanuel: 1137, 1140, 1141
Gaudet, Lazarette: 1035, 1037, 1038, 1419, 1421, 1423
Gaudet, Léo: 1788
Luttrell, Nellie: 347, 349, 352, 353
Maddix, Léah: 715
Perry, Auldine: 1569
Perry, Marcel: 1445
Perry, Rita: 1590, 1705
Pitre, Julienne: 1746
Richard, Madeleine (Mrs. Jérôme Richard): 1267
Richard, Madeleine (Mrs. Lamand Richard): 256

B. Manuscripts

Arsenault, Arcade S.: 125
Arsenault, Frank F.: 202
Arsenault, Joseph J.: 190
Arsenault, Lucille: 212
Chaisson, Maggie: 173
Gallant, Marie-Anne: 3
Letter from Jean Allain to Georges Arsenault regarding Denise Allain, dated
23 February 1996, written in St. Louis, PEI.

Archives of the Archdiocese of Quebec
Letter from Father Antoine Gagnon to Mgr. Joseph-Octave Plessis, dated 21
May 1821, written in Shediac, NB, series 311 NB C. N. 5-54

Archives de Folklore, Université Laval
Antonine Maillet Collection, Recording 152 (Mélanie Arsenault)
Luc Lacourcière Collection, Recording 3606 (Délia Perry)
Roger Matton Collection, Recording 186 (Benoni Benoît)

Public Archives of Prince Edward Island
Letter from Jérôme A. Gallant to J.H. Blanchard, dated 30 March 1931,
written in Collette, NB, J. Henri Blanchard Fonds - 2330, series C-2

Centre d'études acadiennes, Université de Moncton

Bernice Arsenault Collection, Manuscript 29 (Irène Arsenault)
Erma Arsenault Collection, Manuscript 34 (Mrs. Joseph C. Gallant)
Eunice Arsenault, Manuscript 21
Gemma Arsenault Collection, Manuscript 7 (Avis Gallant)
Antoinette DesRoches Collection, Manuscript 46 (Obéline DesRoches)

Centre de recherches acadiennes de l'Île-du-Prince-Édouard, Musée acadien, Miscouche
Souvenirs d'enfance sur l'Île : réponse à Christian. Manuscript, 1986, 72 p., Ozélie Boisvert Fonds - 76
Éveline Poirier Collection, Interview with Marguerita Richard, Société Saint-Thomas-d'Aquin Fonds - S80.6-32

Books

Aarne, Antti and Stith Thompson. *The Types of the Folktale.* Helsinki, Academia Scientiarum Fennica, 1961.

Arsenault, A.E. *Memoirs of the Hon. A.E. Arsenault, Former Premier and Retired Justice, Supreme Court of Prince Edward Island.* Charlottetown, 1951.

Arsenault, Georges. *La chanson du pays.* Summerside, Société Saint-Thomas d'Aquin, 1983.

—. *Complaintes acadiennes de l'Île-du-Prince-Édouard.* Montréal, Leméac, 1980.

—. *Le conte et la légende du pays.* Summerside, Société Saint-Thomas d'Aquin, 1983.

—. *Par un dimanche au soir : Léah Maddix, chanteuse et conteuse acadienne.* Moncton, Éditions d'Acadie, 1993.

Barbeau, Marius. *En roulant ma boule.* Ottawa, Musée national de l'homme, 1982.

Blanchard, J.-Henri. *Rustico : une paroisse acadienne de l'Île-du-Prince-Édouard.* 1937.

Boudreau, Éphrem. *Glossaire du vieux parler acadien.* Montréal, Éditions du Fleuve, 1988.

Butler, Gary R. *Histoire et traditions orales des Franco-Acadiens de Terre-Neuve.* Sillery, Septentrion, 1995.

Creighton, Helen. *Chansons folkloriques d'Acadie. La fleur du rosier. Acadian Folksongs.* Edited by Ronald Labelle. Sydney, University College of Cape Breton Press, 1988.

Delarue, Paul. *Le conte populaire français.* Vol. 1. Paris, Éditions Érasme, 1957.

Delarue, Paul and Marie-Louise Tenèse. *Le conte populaire français.* Paris, Éditions G.-P. Maisonneuve et Larose, Vol. 2, 1964, Vol. 3, 1976.

Dictionnaire des oeuvres littéraires du Québec. Vol. 1. Edited by Maurice Lemire. Montréal, Fides, 1978.

Dupont, Jean-Claude. *Le légendaire de la Beauce.* Québec, Éditions Garneau, 1974.

Église Immaculée Conception, Palmer Road 1892–1992. Palmer Road, 1992.

Gallant, Antoinette. *Little Jack an' de Tax-Man.* Bedeque, Elaine Harrison & Associates, 1979.

Gallant, Cécile. *Le mouvement coopératif chez les Acadiens de la région Évangéline (1862–1982).* Wellington, Conseil coopératif de l'Île-du-Prince-Édouard, 1982.

Gallant, Patrice. *Michel Haché-Gallant et ses descendants.* Vol. 1. Sayabec, self-published, 1970.

Jolicoeur, Catherine. *Les plus belles légendes acadiennes.* Montréal, Stanké, 1981.

Laforte, Conrad. *Le catalogue de la chanson folklorique française.* 6 volumes. Québec, Presses de l'Université Laval, 1977–1987.

—. *Menteries dôles et merveilleuses : contes traditionnels du Saguenay.* Montréal, Éditions Quinze, 1978.

LeBlanc, Émery. *La vie à Sainte-Marie.* n.p., 1984.

Léger, Lauraine. *Les sanctions populaires en Acadie.* Montréal, Leméac, 1978.

Lemieux, Germain. *Les jongleurs du billochet.* Montréal, Bellarmin, 1972.

Pineau, Léon. *Le folklore du Poitou.* Poitiers, Le Bouquiniste, 1977 (first published c.1892).

Proulx, J.-B. *L'enfant perdu et retrouvé ou Cholet.* Montréal, Beauchemin, 1949.

Poirier, Pascal. *Le glossaire acadien.* Edited by Pierre M. Gérin. Moncton, Éditions d'Acadie, 1994.

Ramsay, Sterling. *Folklore: Prince Edward Island.* Charlottetown, Square Deal Publications.

Thomas, Gerald. *Les deux traditions: le conte populaire chez les Franco-Terreneuviens.* Montréal, Bellarmin, 1983.

Thompson, Stith. *The Folktale.* Berkeley, University of California Press, 1977.

Articles

Arsenault, Georges. "Xavier Gallant." *Dictionary of Canadian Biography.* Vol. 5. Toronto, University of Toronto, 1983.

—. "La chanson locale et l'histoire sociale acadienne." *La Petite Souvenance,* No. 13 (Dec. 1985), pp. 8–22.

—. "Les chansons acadiennes de composition locale." *Canadian Folk Music Journal,* Vol. 9 (1981), pp. 20–33.

—."Chanter son Acadie." *Vie française*, Québec, Conseil de la vie française en Amérique, 1984, pp. 101–110.

—."La Marlèche conte-type 56B." *Culture & Tradition*, Vol. 1 (1976), pp. 19-31.

Cormier, Charlotte."Les aspects musicaux de la chanson locale acadienne." *Les Acadiens : état de la recherche*, Québec, Conseil de la vie française en Amérique, 1987, pp. 76–107.

Jolicoeur, Catherine."Légendes acadiennes." *Revue de l'Université Laurentienne*, Vol. 8, No. 2 (Feb. 1976), pp. 21–29.

MacEachern, Alan Andrew."Theophilus Stewart and the Plight of the Micmacs." *The Island Magazine*, No. 28 (Fall/Winter 1990), pp. 3–11.

Pineau, Wilfred."Contes et légendes de chez nous." *Album souvenir des fêtes du bicentenaire chez les Acadiens de l'Île-du-Prince-Édouard, 1755–1955*, Charlottetown, 1955, pp. 11–12.

Saint-Hildebert (Sister) [Annie White]."La sorcellerie." *La Petite Souvenance*, No. 12 (June 1985), pp. 25–26.

Newspapers

The Examiner
"Tignish Notes," 12 August 1889, p. 2.

The Islander (supplement, *The Guardian*)
Drake, Carolyn."Ghost Stories Can Be Found Everywhere." 23 June 1990, p. 5.
—."Rural Island Lifestyle Perfect for Ghostly Tales." 23 June 1990, p. 5.
Porter, Marcia."Ghost Stories Common to P.E.I." 23 June 1990, p. 3.
—."Phantom Ships." 23 June 1990, p. 6.

The Journal-Pioneer
"Abram's Village Plant to Open." 10 August 1971.
"Lazarette Gaudet Dies at 82." 18 January 1902.
"Obituary - Joseph Alyre Chaisson." 27 January 1994.

L'Impartial
"La paroisse de Cascumpec." 17 March 1904, p. 3.
"Un trésor serait caché au 'North Cape'." 29 March 1906, p. 1.
[Laurent Doucet]. 3 May 1893, p. 3.

The Patriot
"Drowned [Sylvain Caissie]. 23 July 1901.

La Voix acadienne
[Antoinette Gallant]. "Rustico : on raconte." 14 July 1976, p. 8.

Recordings
Acadie et Québec. RCA Victor, CGP-139.
Butler, Édith. *Asteur qu'on est là...* SPPS, PS-199905, 1979.
—. *Édith Butler à Paquetville*. SPPS, PS-199911, 1980.
—. *Édith Butler à Paris*. Disques Kappa, KP-1111, 1983.
Comment ça flippe. Les productions de l'Île, Île-1002, 1981.
Le temps de vivre. Vol. 1, SELECT, SSP-24.246.
Voyage musical Québec. Auvidis/Silex 94, YA-225705.

About the cover

Sunburst (24"x33") by Karen Gallant is an acrylic painting of a North Shore fishing village in Prince Edward Island, close to where painter Karen Gallant grew up. One of the images from her childhood that has stayed with her is this one, showing salted fish hanging out to dry in the sun before it is stored for winter.

Karen Gallant is a graphic artist and illustrator from Rustico, who now lives in Charlottetown. Her paintings can be found at Great Northern Knitters in downtown Charlottetown, and in galleries across the Island.